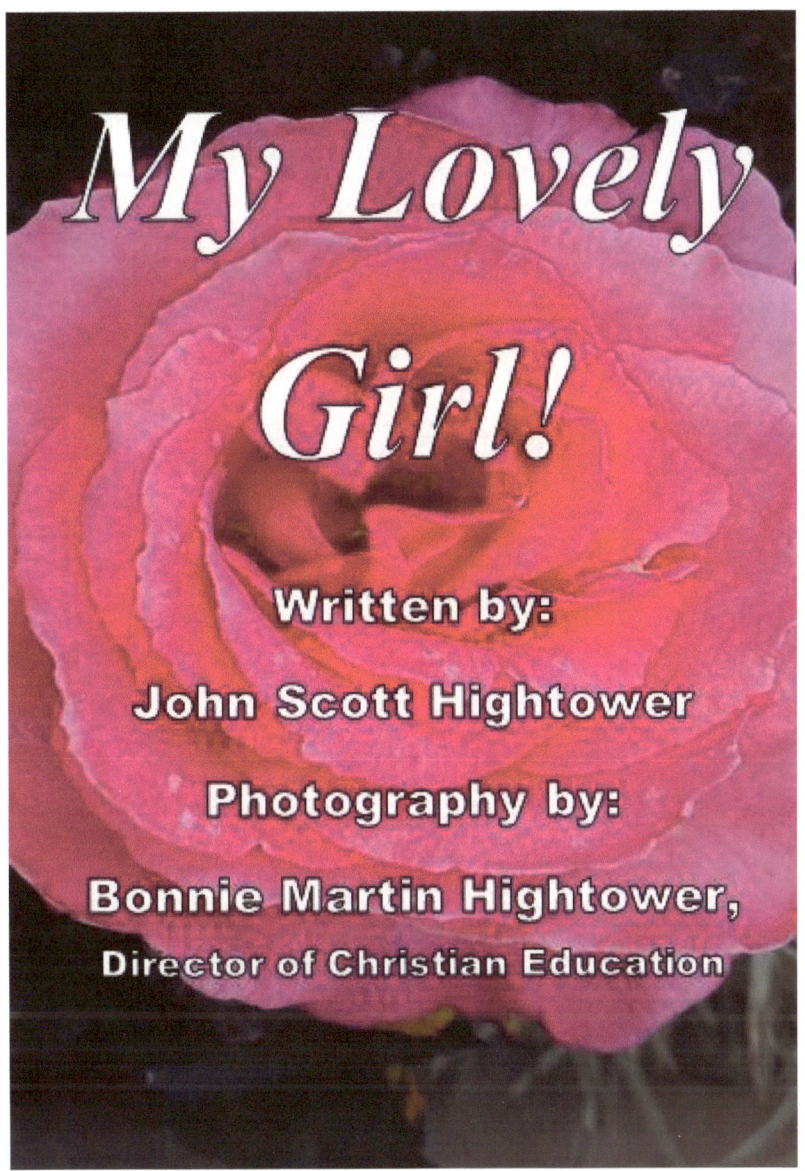

CreateSpace Independent Publishing Platform/Publishers
North Charleston, SC

My Lovely Girl!

Copyright © 2019 by Glad We Thought of It
Revision: September 19, 2019
All rights reserved

Published in the United States by CreateSpace Independent Publishing Platform/Publishers

Library of Congress Cataloging-in-Publication Date

Hightower, Bonnie & John Scott

Glad We Thought of It / Bonnie & John Scott Hightower

ISBN: 9781795674324

Printed in United States

Book and jacket photographs by Bonnie Martin Hightower

My Lovely Girl!

My Lovely Girl!

My Lovely Girl!

Dedication

To my dearest, darling, wife Bonnie. You are the only reason I write love poems. Thanks for helping to open up my heart.

-From my heart to your heart!

My Lovely Girl!

Table of Content

- My Lovely Girl
- I see thousands of flowers on the ground
- A simple smile
- My Love is beautiful
- Words come from the heart to the brain
- A flower is a thing of beauty
- A healthy amount of heat
- Always know I Love You
- Birds chirp as the sun rises higher
- Don't let the world get you down and demoralized
- Flowers bloom as rain pours
- I am completely satisfied
- I am set the rest of my life with you in it
- There is an old song
- My thoughts always come back to you
- Shine
- Rainbows shine beautiful
- Like all the natural wonders of the world
- Love is us
- My heart always rings yours
- When I see your smile
- Love you and I
- Missing you is not a problem
- Love Passion
- Live and love life

My Lovely Girl!

Table of Content (Cont'd)

- For the color and beauty
- Love is in the air
- There will be no fancy words
- You make me
- Remember Love Always heals
- There will be no admiring from a far
- Love is our business
- Love is a fabulous word
- Loving you is hotsy, totsy red
- The heavens called and we listened
- I hope I am your Rock
- I came out of the stratosphere
- You are so delicately beautiful
- There is this story
- The wind is blowing through our hair
- Love is strength
- When I asked if you wanted
- Love is long as love is sure
- You and me together
- Upon our first kiss you awoke my spirit
- Star dust and fairy tales
- Intertwined our love has become
- That wink and glimmer in your eyes
- Love is like the sun coming
- 1 Corinthians 13:13

My Lovely Girl!

Forward

My dearest, darling, wife Bonnie:

You and I were destined to be together. From the day you walked into the place I worked, I knew. We started talking that day, and we still haven't stopped. I hope that I have helped you, as much as, you have helped me. I love you tremendously and every line of poetry I write is full of love, from me to you. Thank you for joining me on our journey!

-From my heart to your heart!

My Lovely Girl!

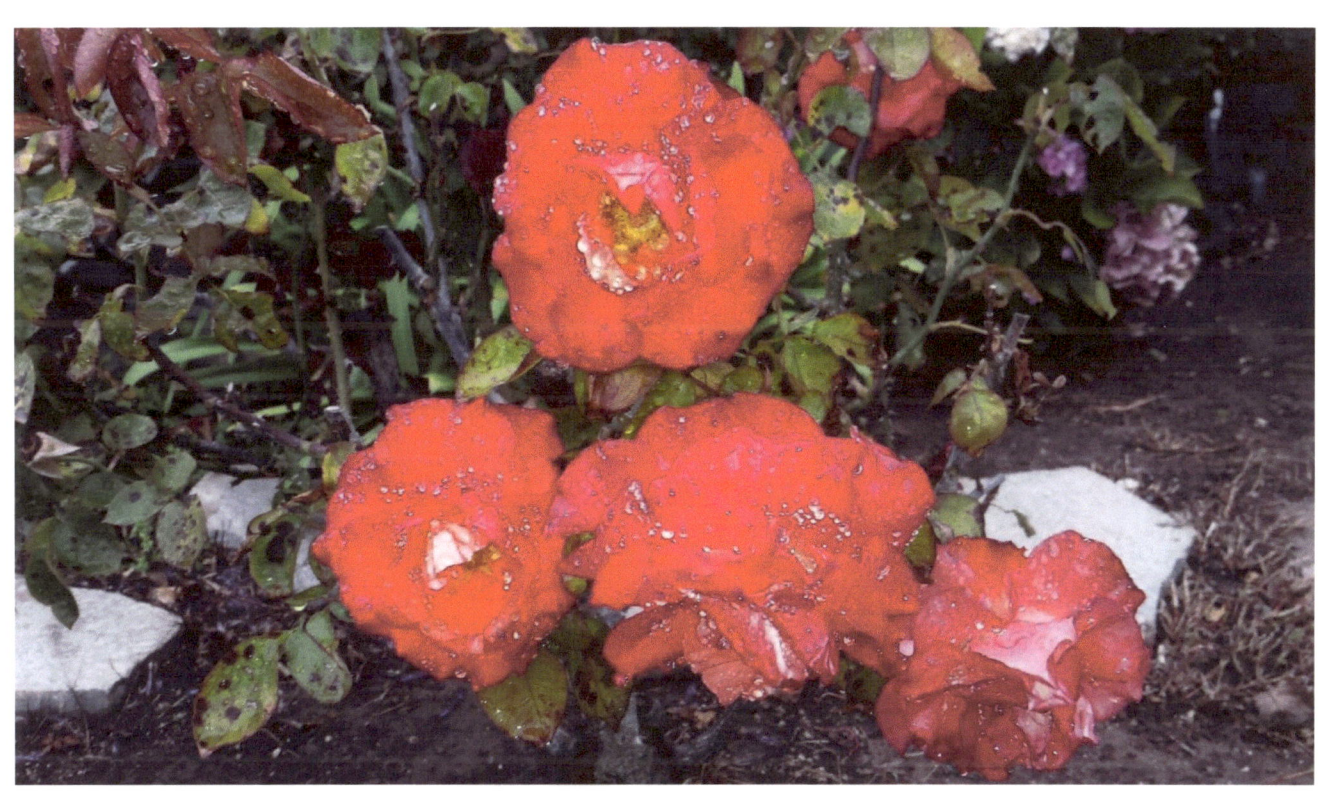

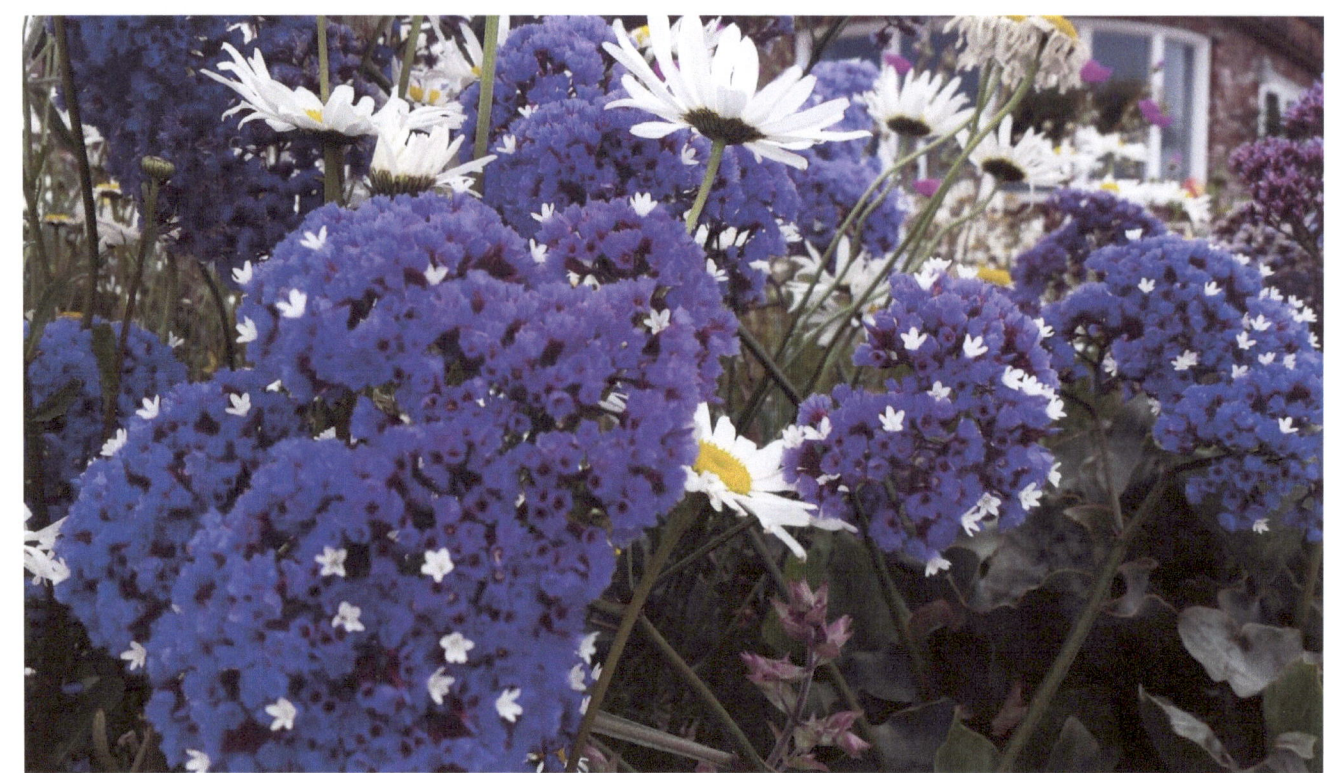

I see thousands of flowers on the ground
in the trees, hanging from peoples
porches and thousands of gardens
throughout the world
In beautiful displays in restaurants,
on the lapel of lovers going to a dance
but none of
these have any hold on the beauty that I
see every morning, afternoon and night
when I am blessed to
gaze upon your gorgeous face

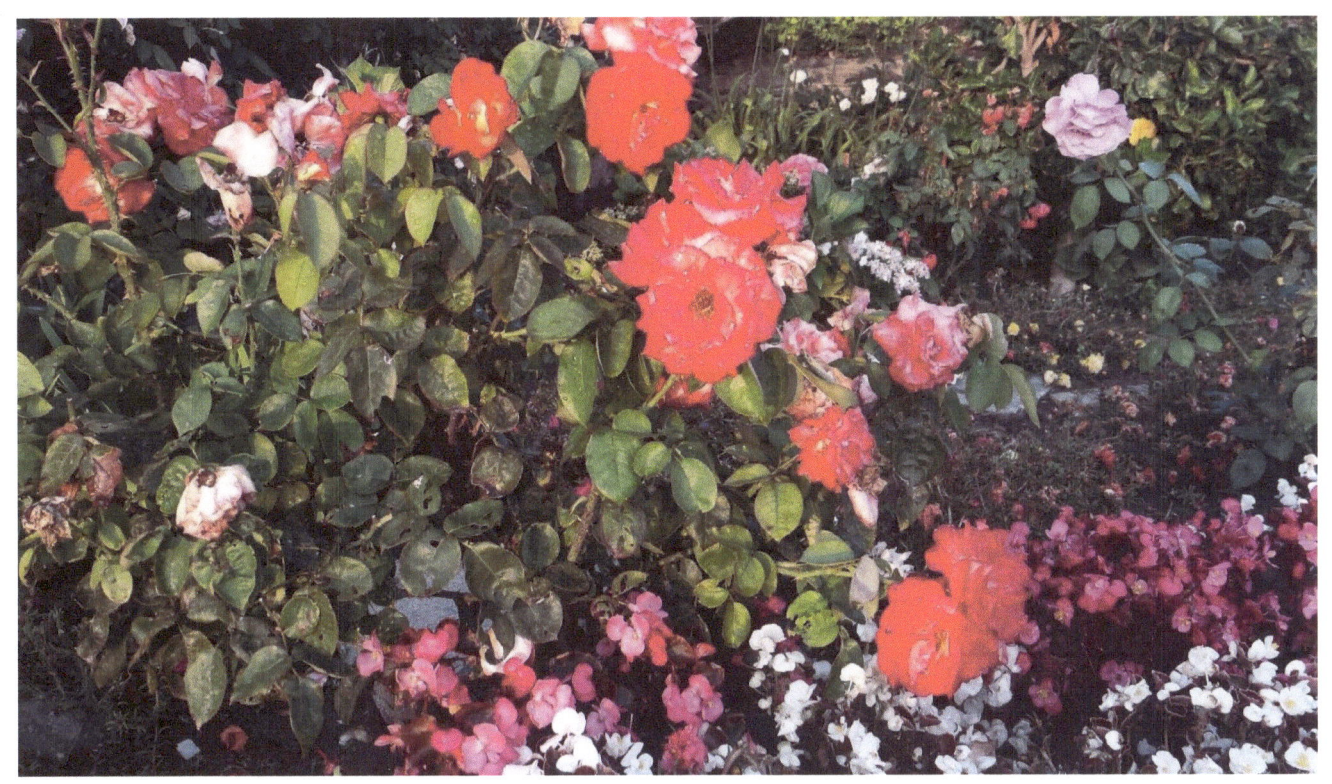

A simple smile could make a whole world of difference to a person you cross on the street. Just think if it would brighten your day, think of the person you smile at.

Imagine I'm smiling at you!

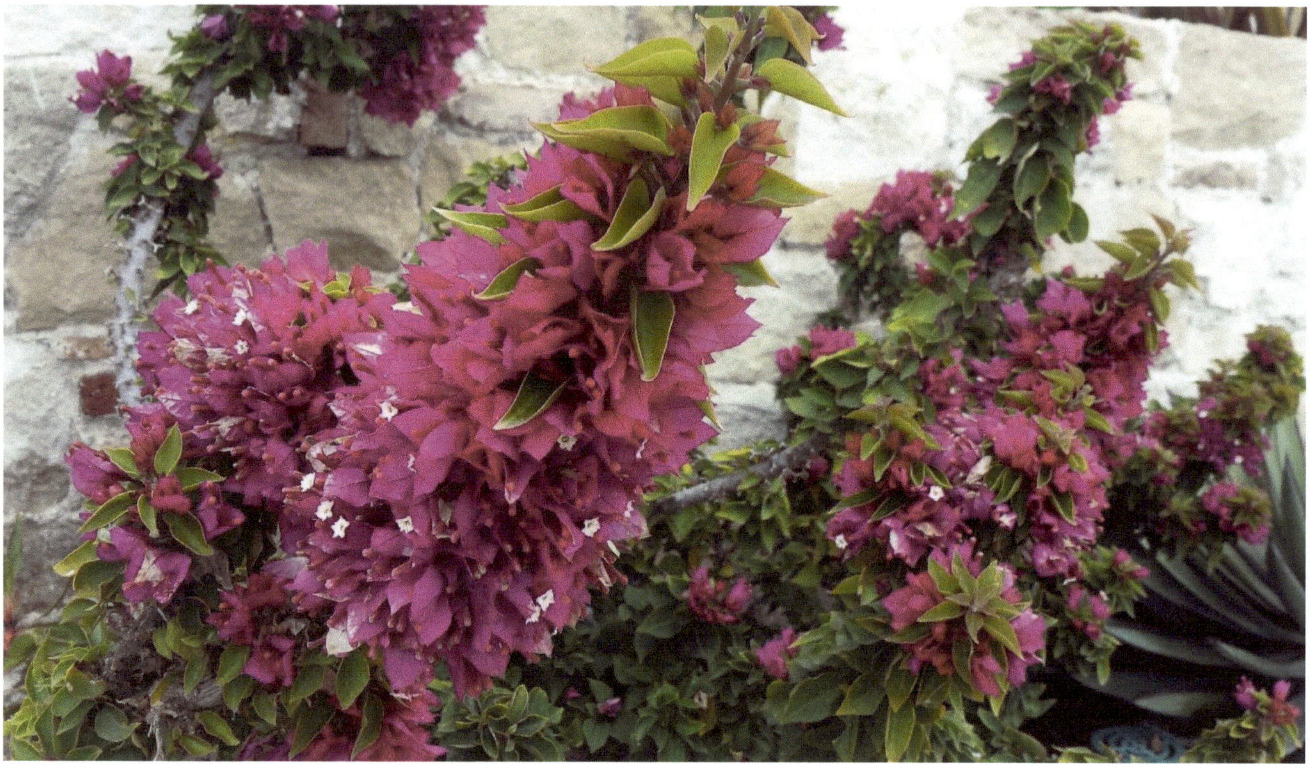

My Love is beautiful

so I choose beautiful words

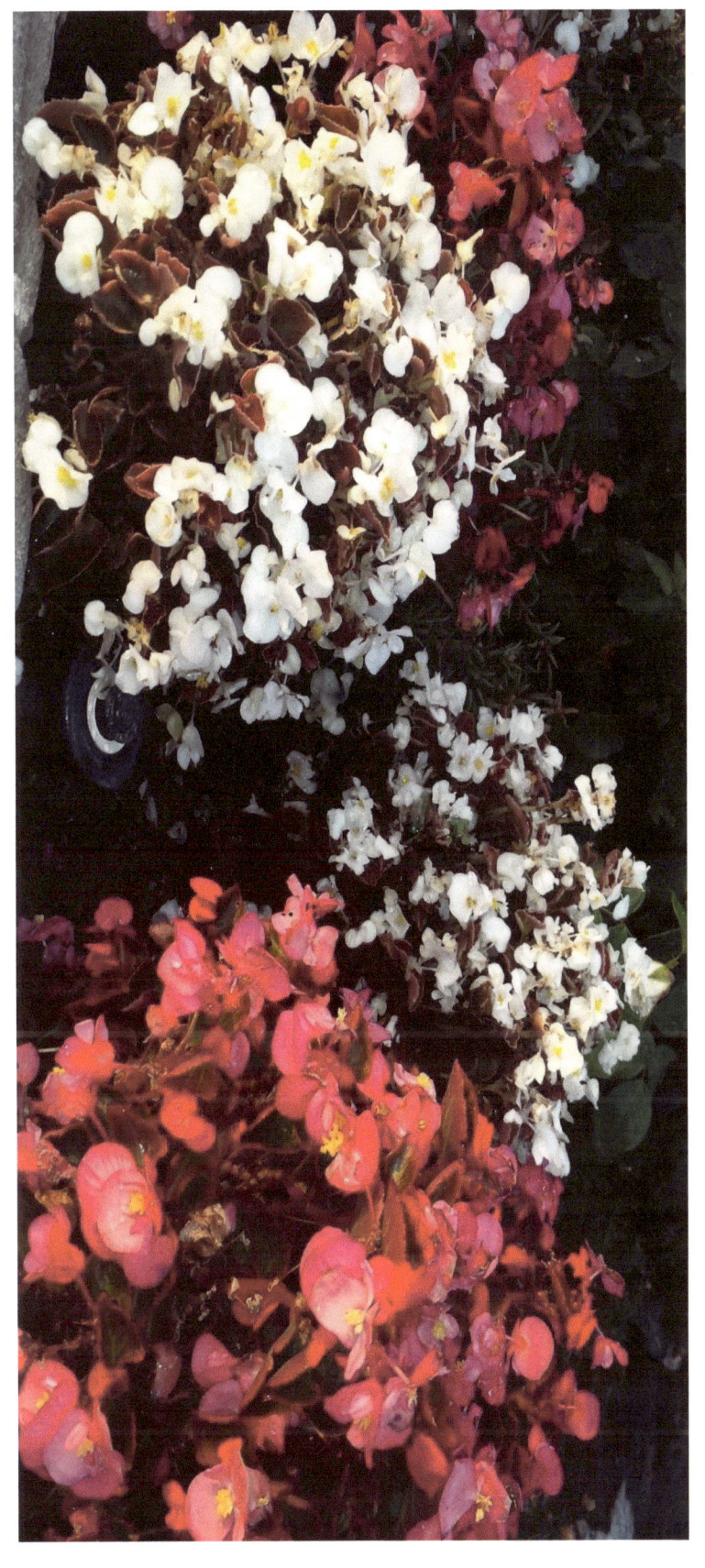

Words come
from the heart
to the brain
down through
fingers
unto paper
some are
victorian
others poetic
and the rest
could be
scribbles
mine to you
are all the above
Love is in every
word!

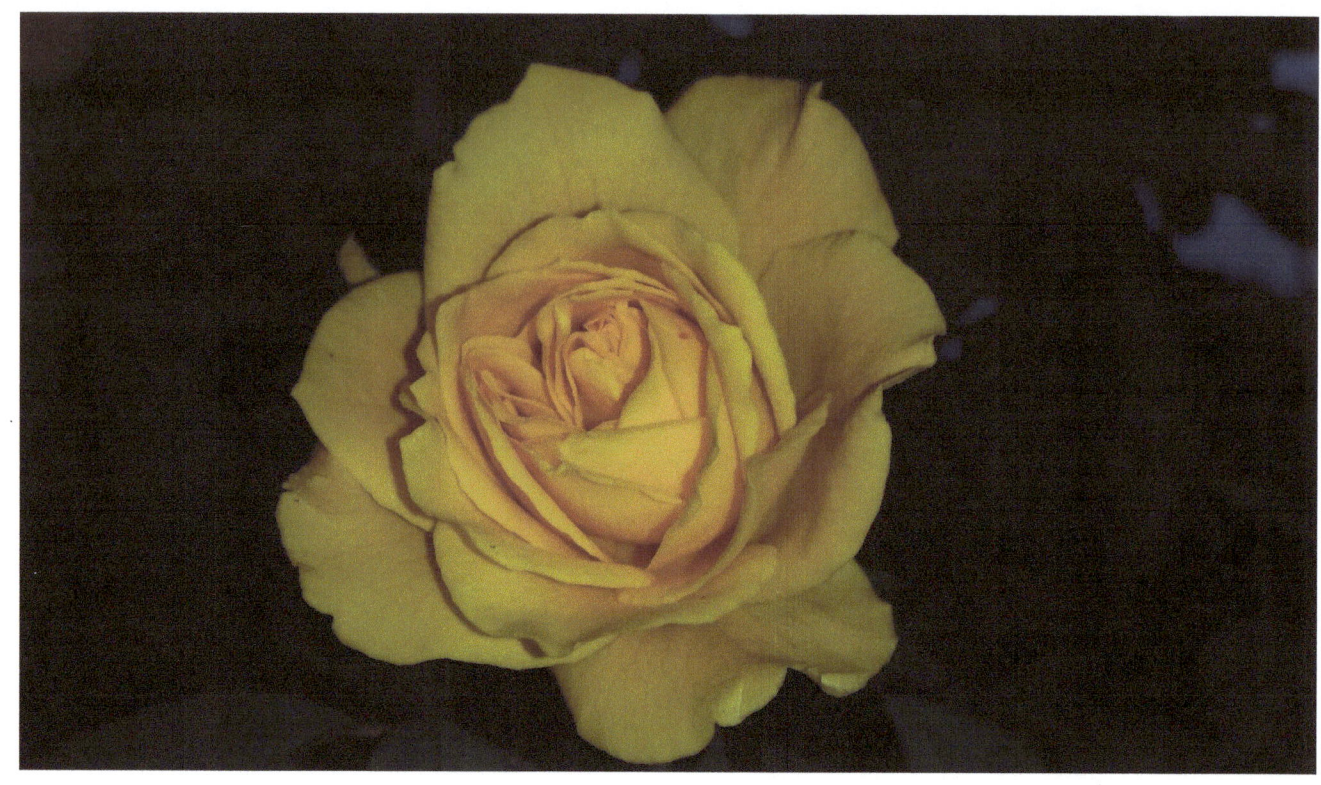

A flower is a thing of beauty
That the eye can see and
the nose can smell
You are a thing of beauty
That my eye can see and my
heart can feel

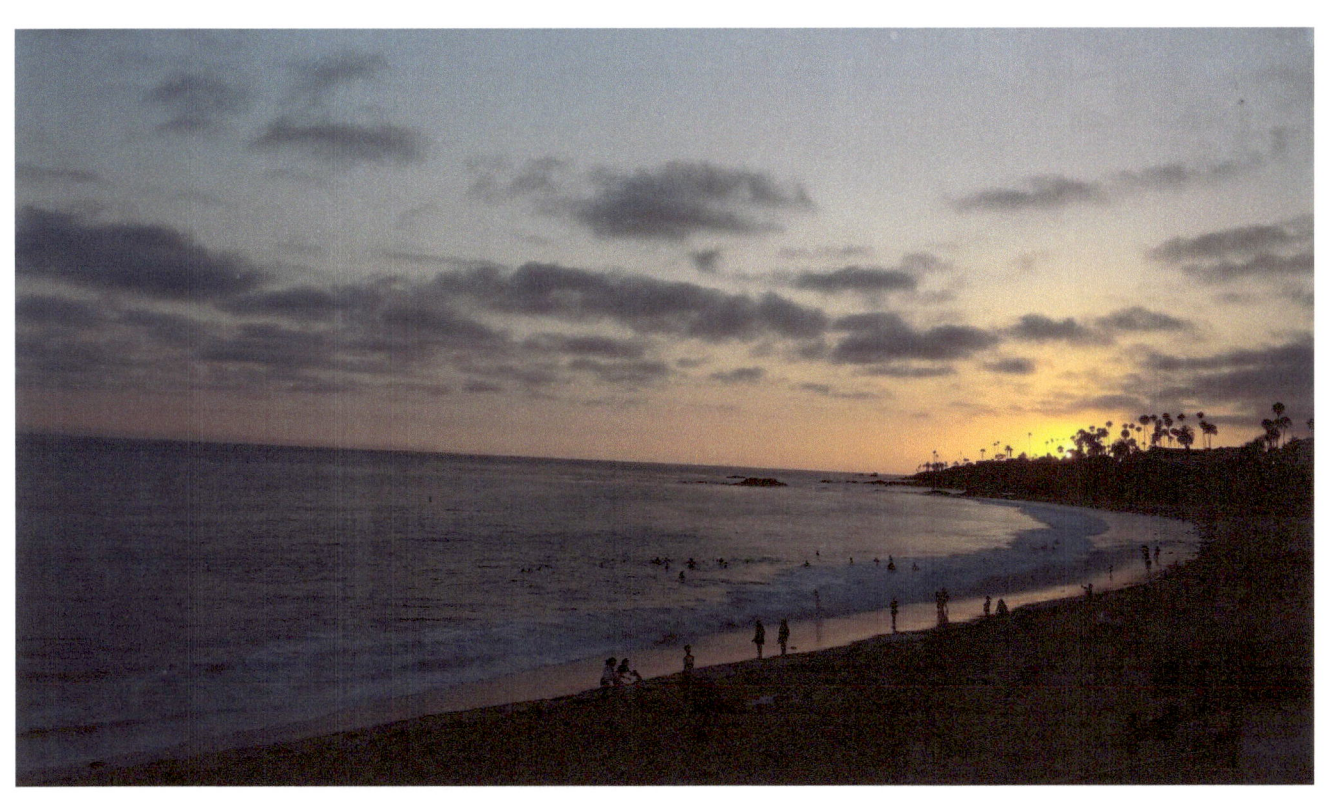

A healthy amount of heat
is what I get when
I think of You,
Standing next to You,
holding You,
and basically
everything we do
together ♡♡♡

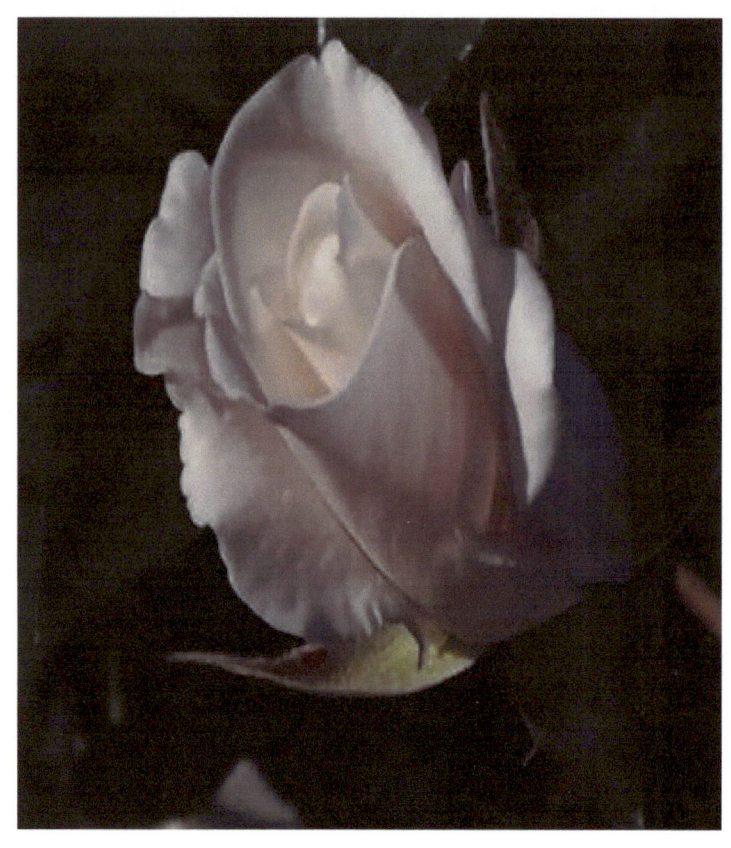

**Always know
I Love You,
and You are my Truth!**

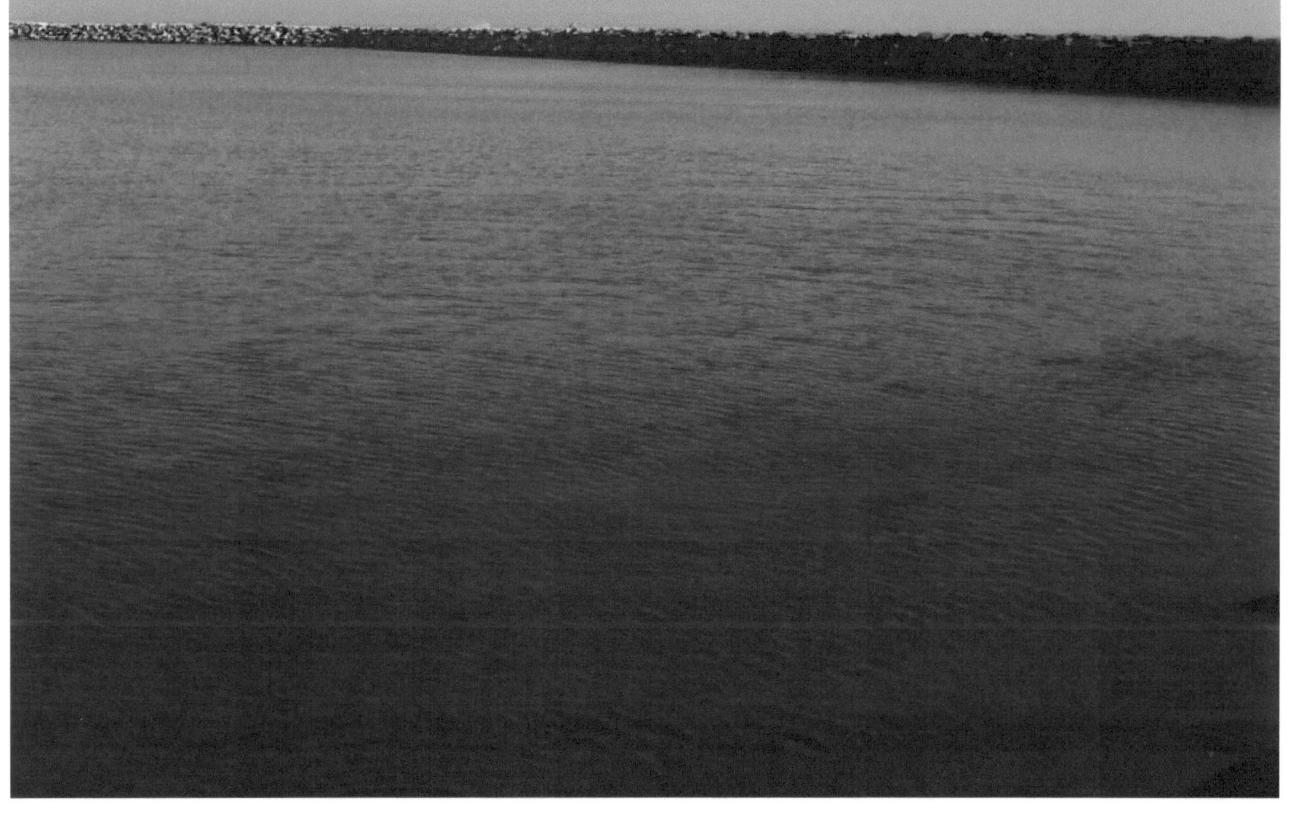

Birds chirp as the sun rises higher
Butterflies float as the wind settles across the land
Worms inch along as the soaked ground dries
Eagles fly high and proud over a still and quiet land
Salmon swim up river to begin life
Deer run by to show their grace
Rabbits hop by out of sheer glee
Dolphins jump for joy in the warm calming oceans
As all this takes place in nature just know our Love
will Always be there to help the sun shine

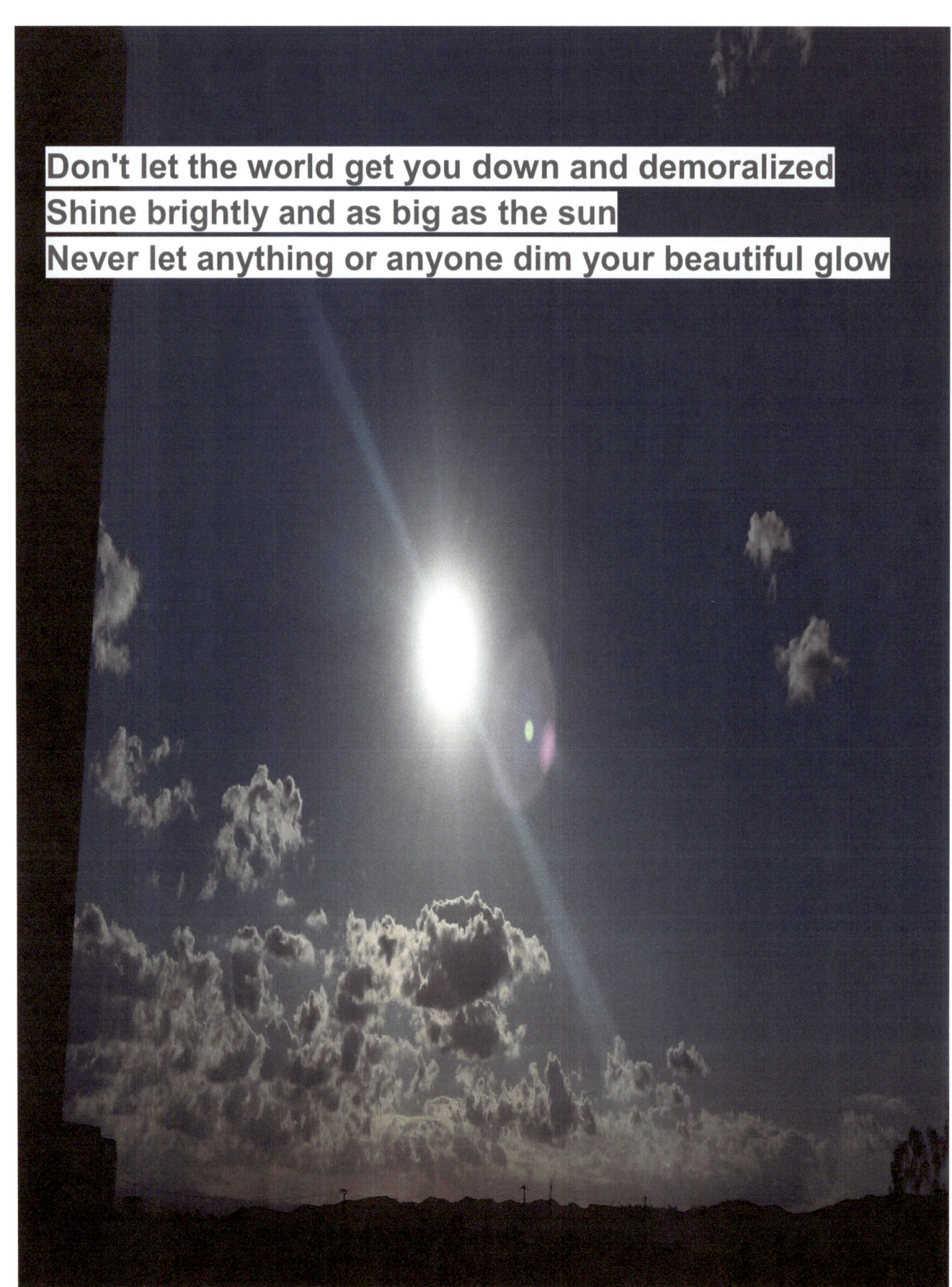

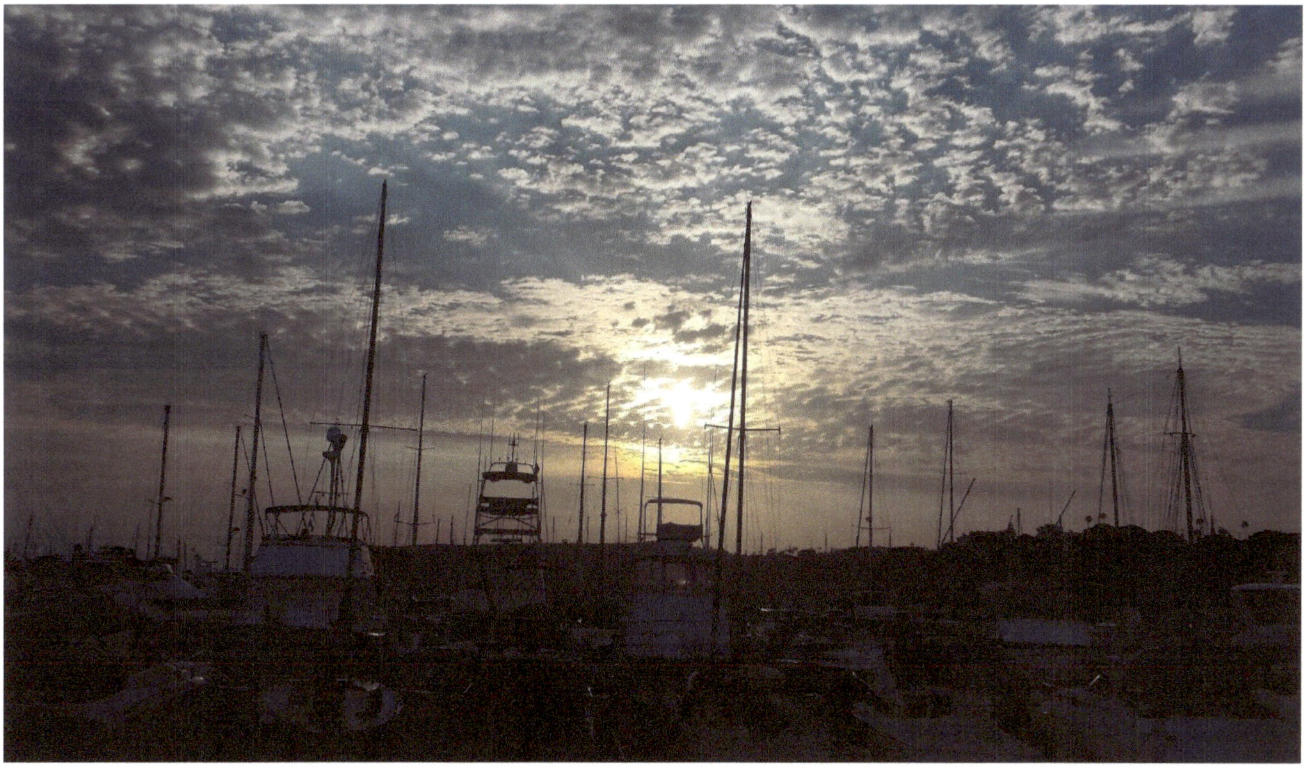

Even during the cloudiest,
darkest,
dizziest,
wettest,
longest,
rainiest,
scariest
days
You are the loveliest in my heart.

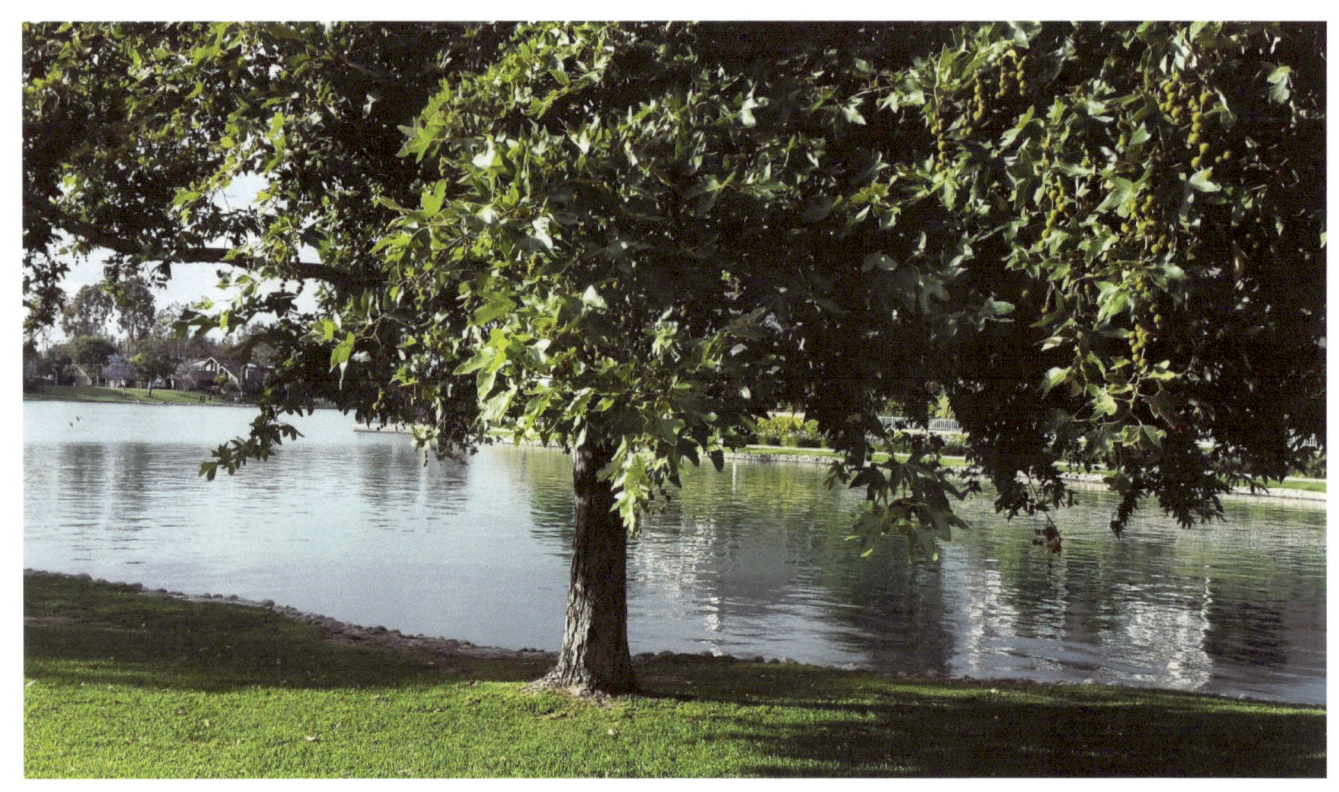

Flowers bloom as rain pours

Blades of grass turn green as the dew sets

Trees grow tall so they can touch the blue crystal sky

Leaves fall to the ground to warm the earth

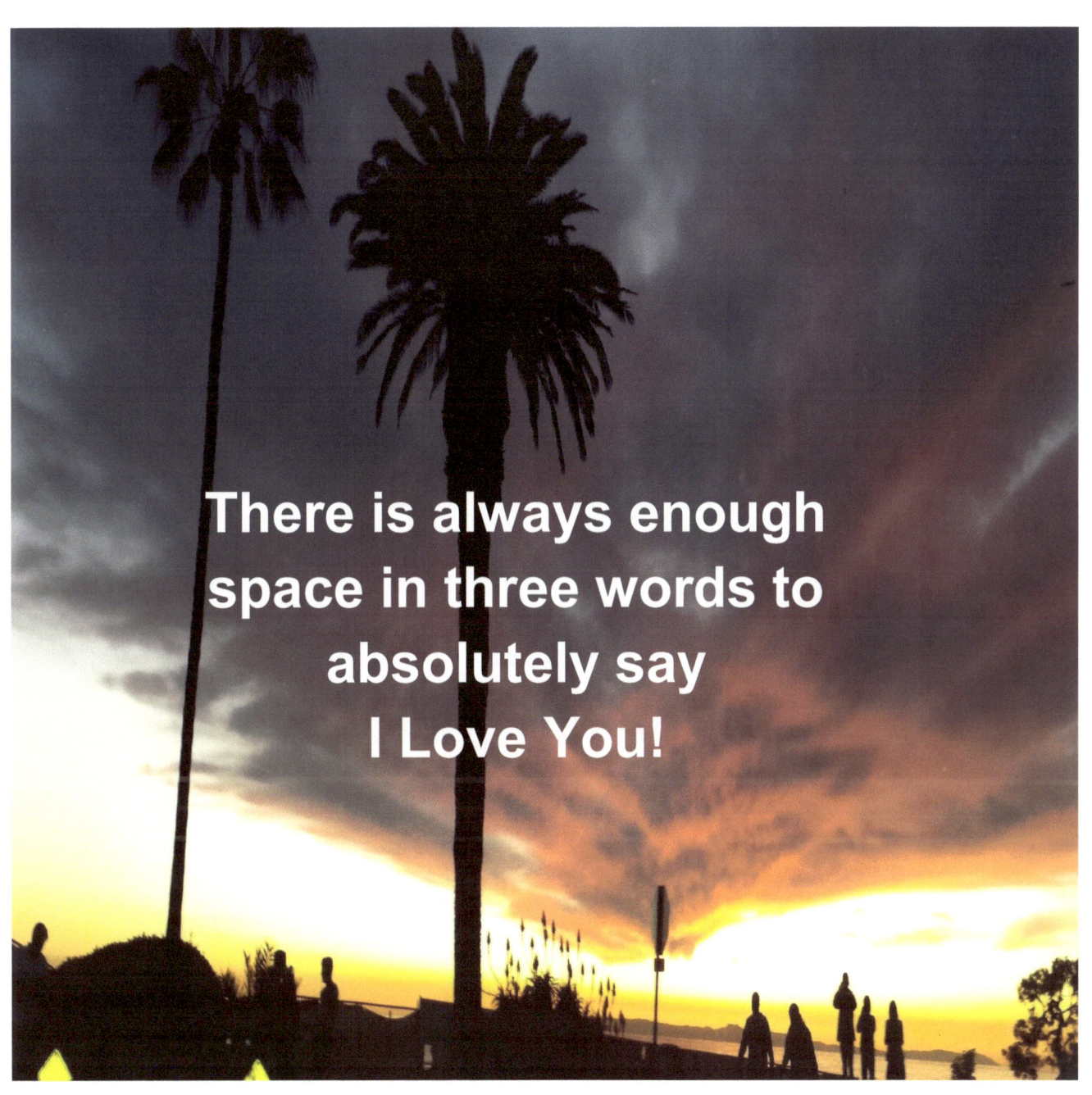

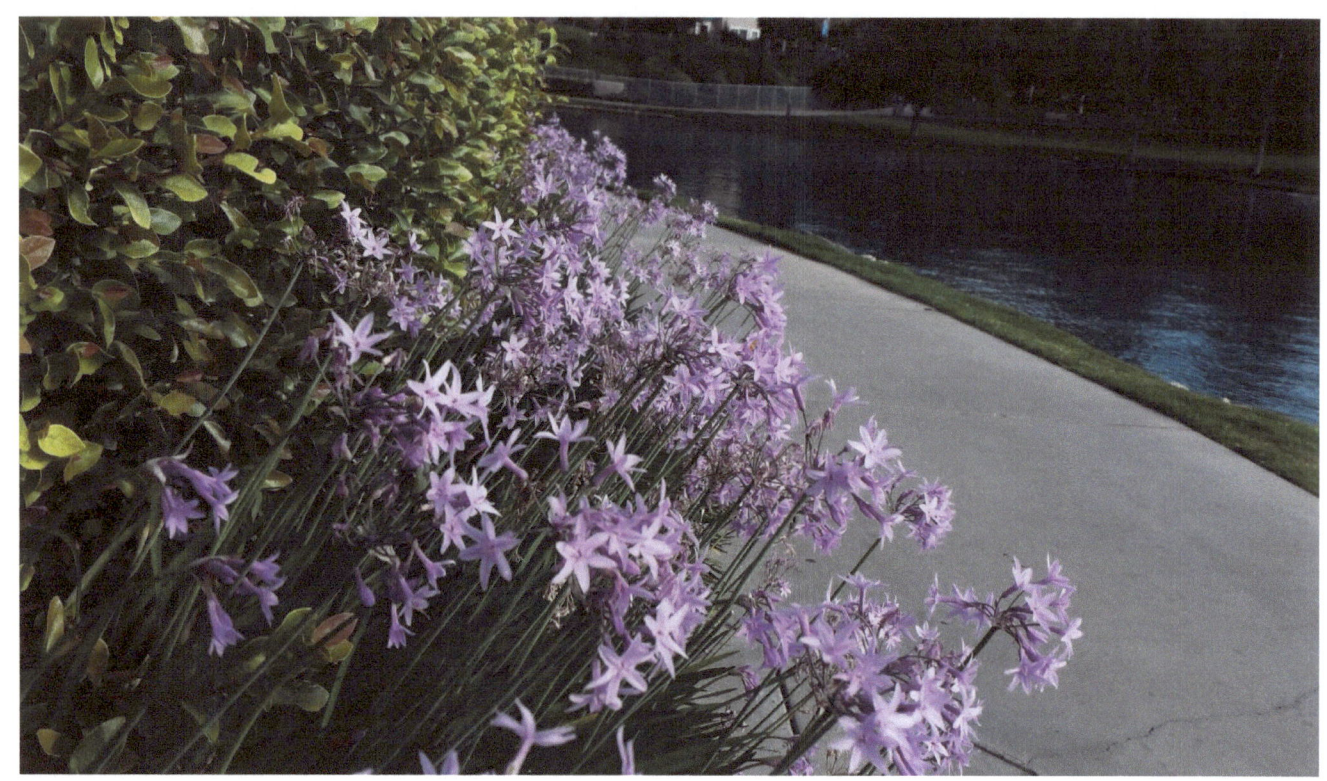

I am completely satisfied,
content, happy and excited
(if you know what I mean)
with You.

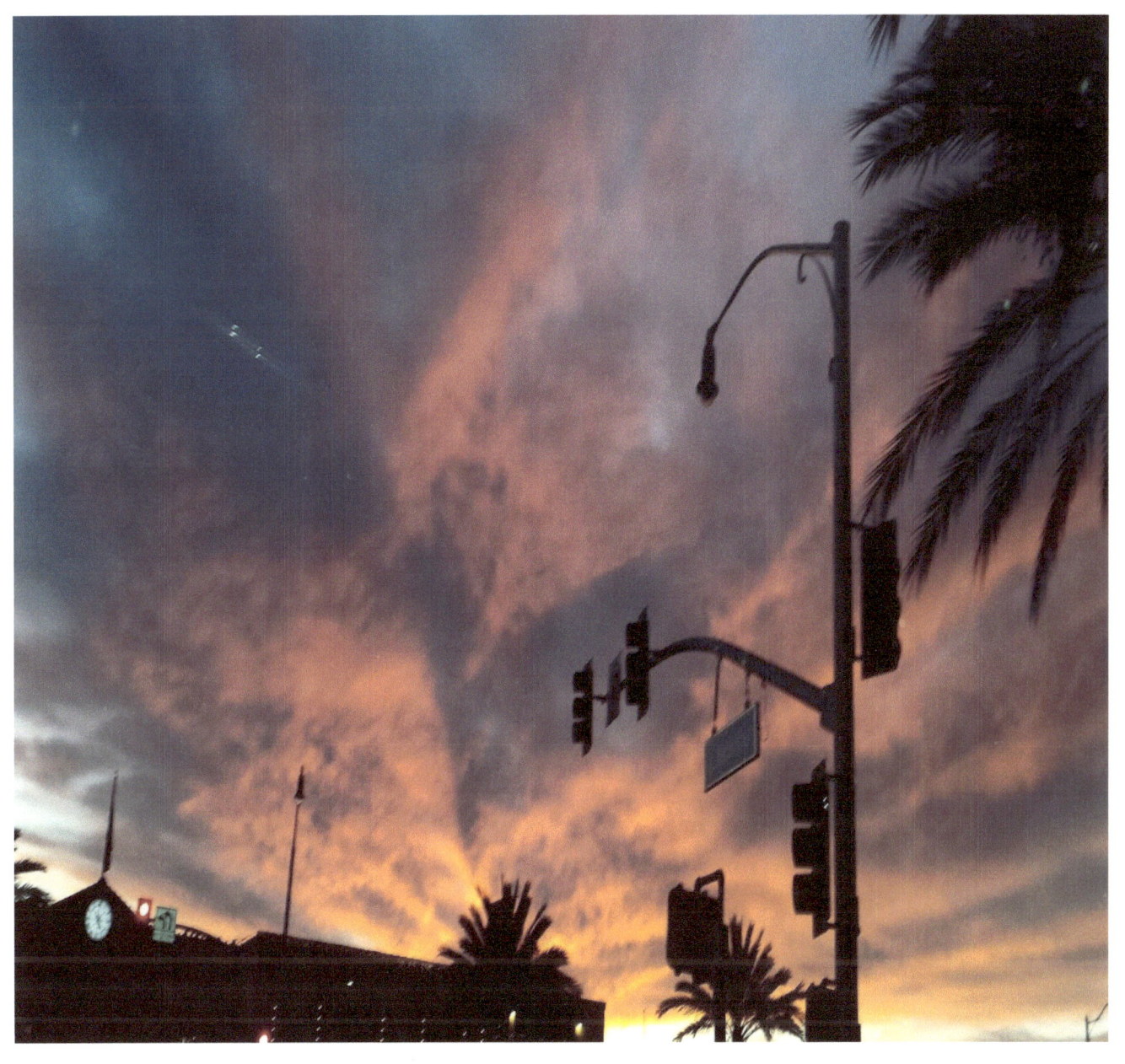

I am set the rest of my life with you in it.

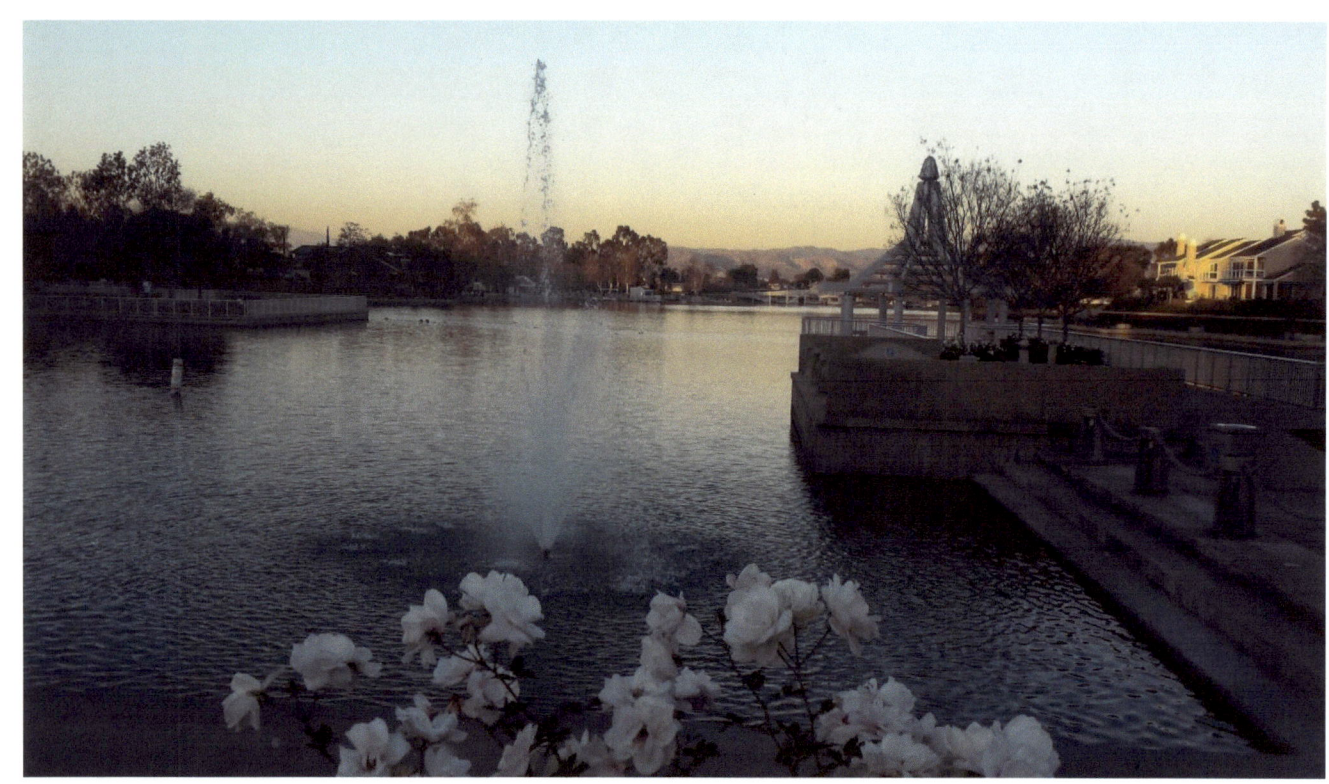

My thoughts always come back to you
That shows a true sign of a **Love**
that has no bounds
Is not confined to one or several
centuries and over time the **Love** is there
for everyone to see and to share but for
now my eyes, my heart and my fingers
only belong to you

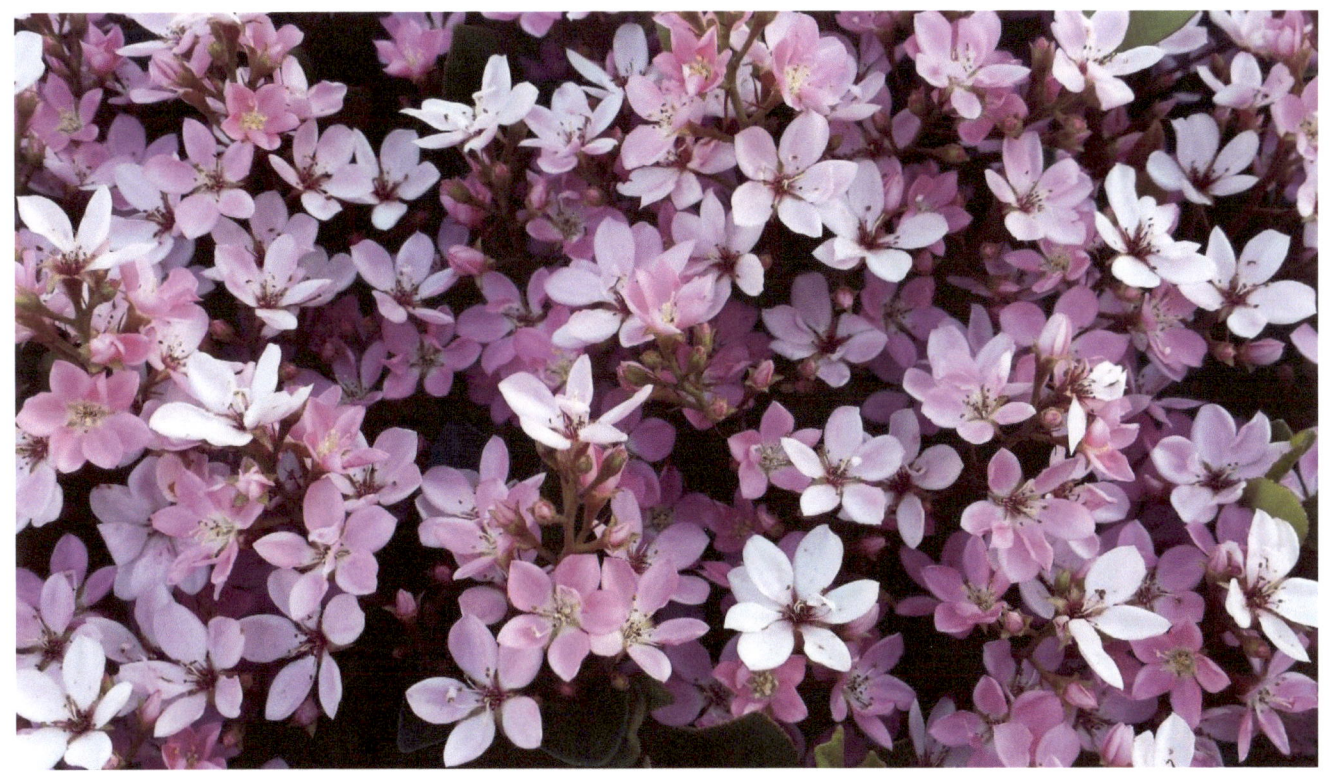

There is an old song, "You light up my life"
Well in your case
I am on fire because of you
You light me up
Every fiber of my being is shining
I'm afraid for when we hug the electricity will shoot us to the moon
First I must thank God for giving you everything you have on your inside as well as out
Well I am a man and I appreciate the fine artistry God did with putting you together
Most of all I thank you for all your inwardly beauty
You define the term – Loving and Caring person
Keep up the fireworks and we shall share a rocket to the outer reaches of the universe

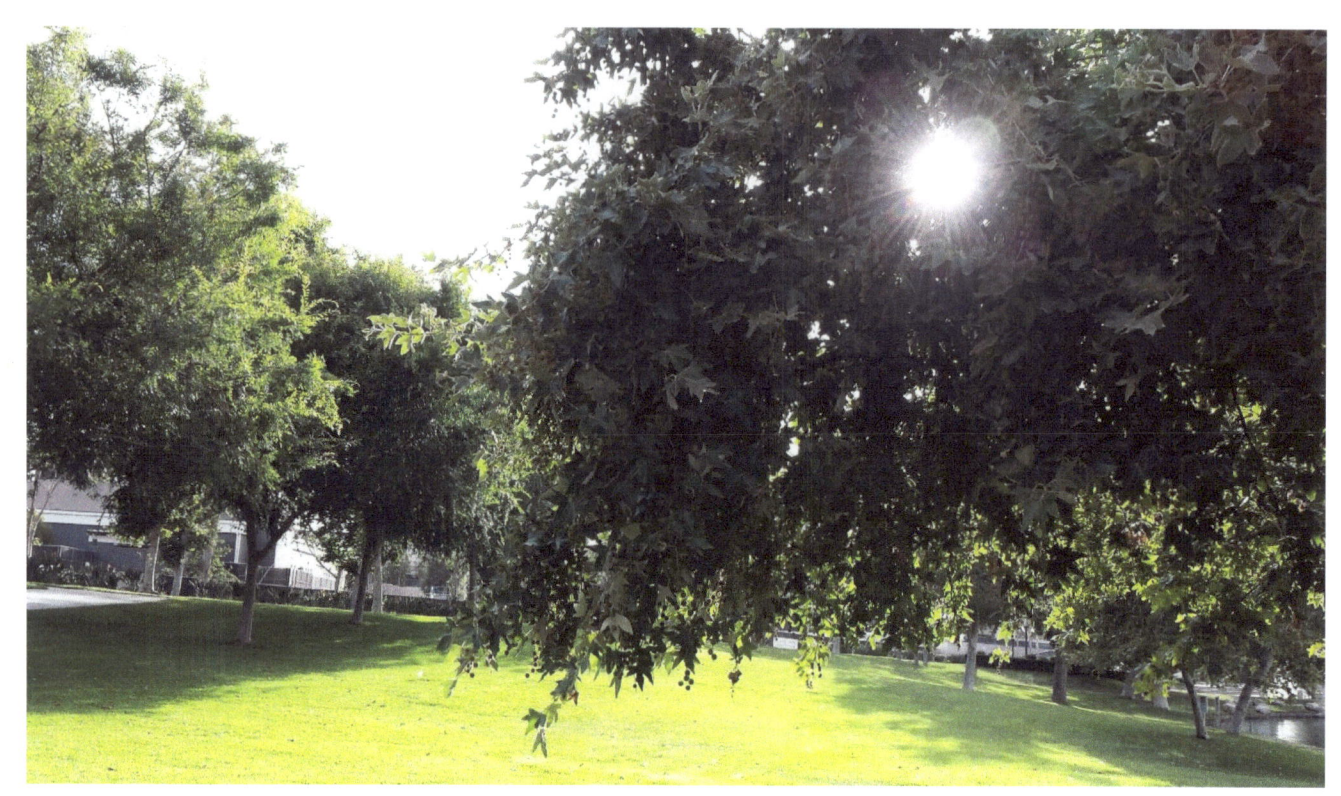

Shine ever so brightly my dear.

For you are my bright shining star!

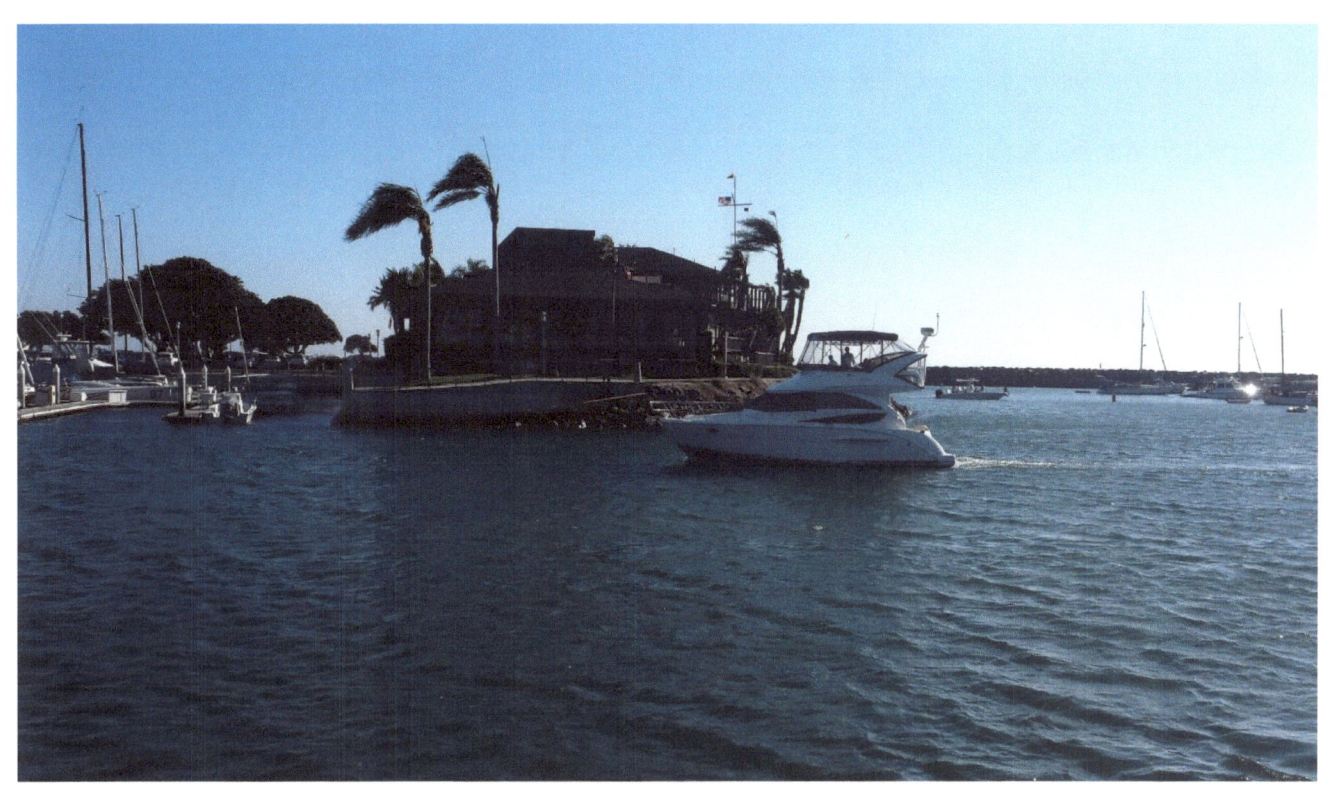

Rainbows shine beautiful, colorful lights to brighten the day
Sun rays hug people to give them energy
Wind blows to clear the sky and our minds
Rain washes out the old so the new can grow
As does our Love help the flowers thrive

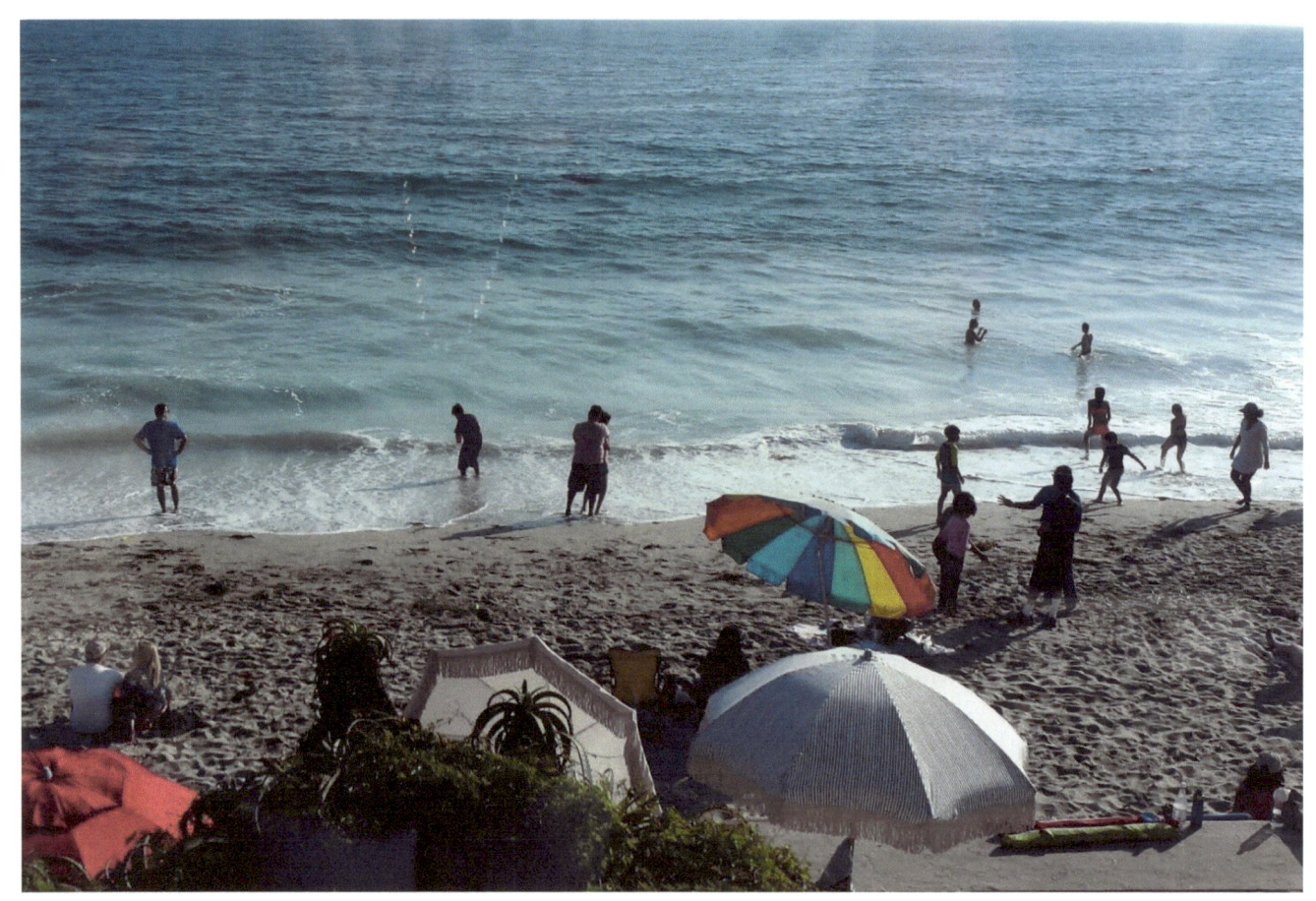

Like all the natural wonders of the world

God placed you on earth

God brought us together to show harmony is still in the air

Our love gains strength because

You are one of God's natural wonders

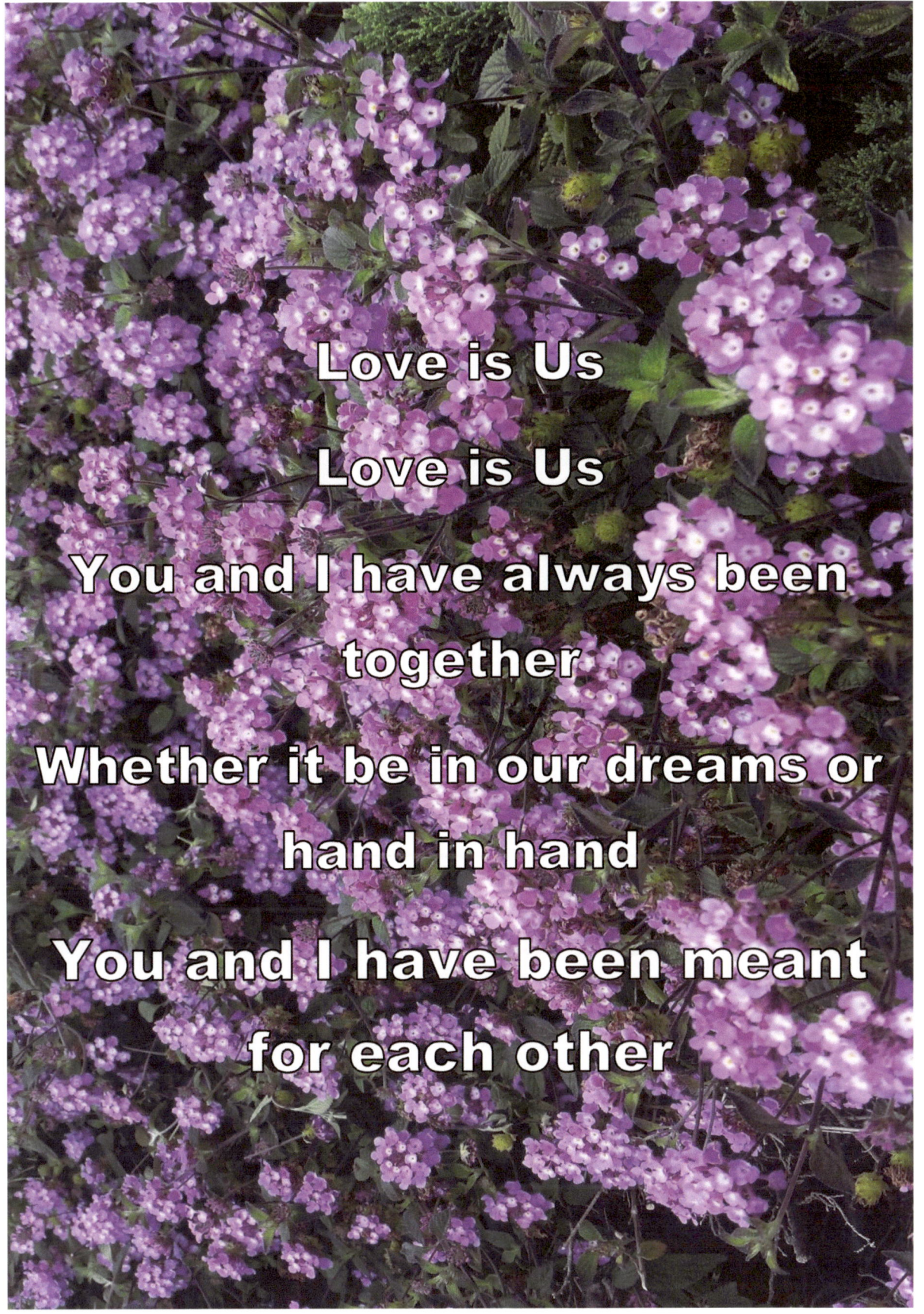

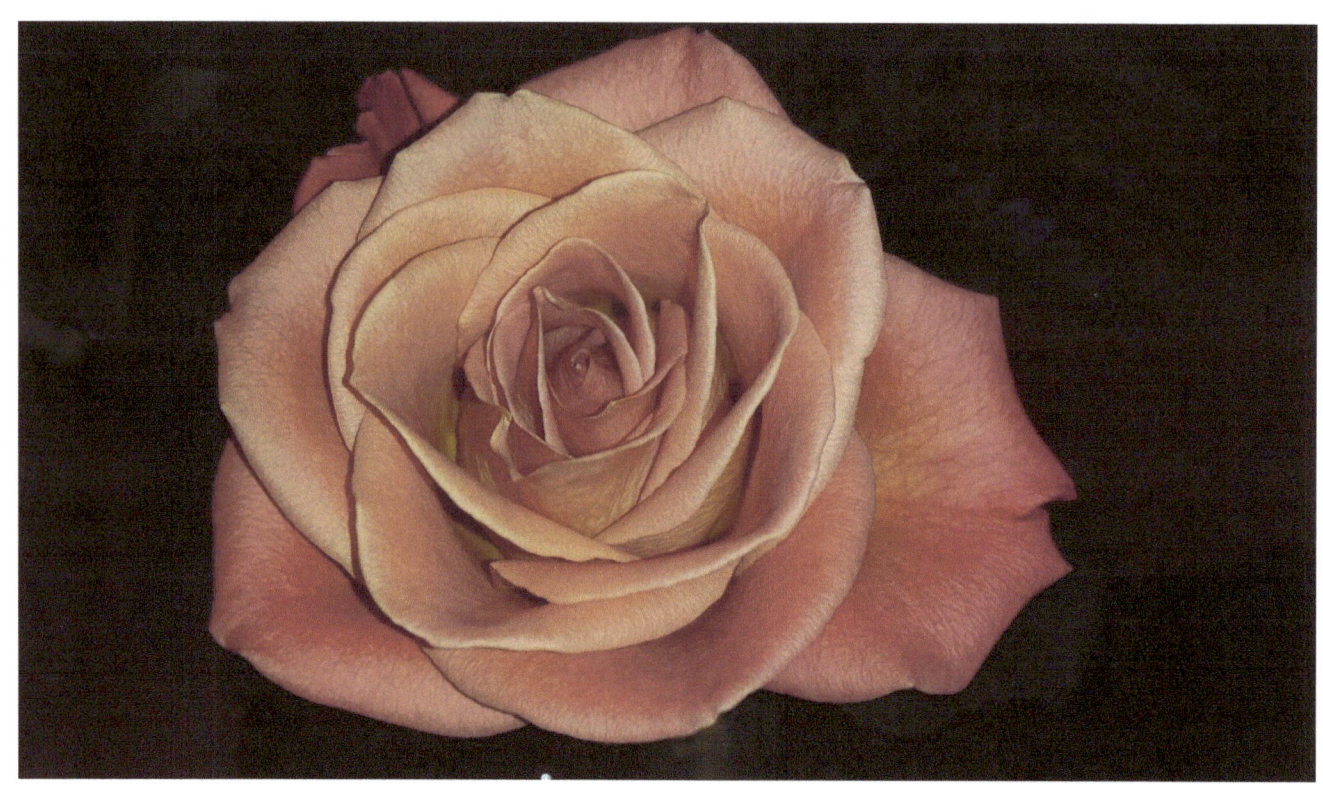

My heart rings yours every second of the day. Thanks for Always picking up and keeping our connection strong.

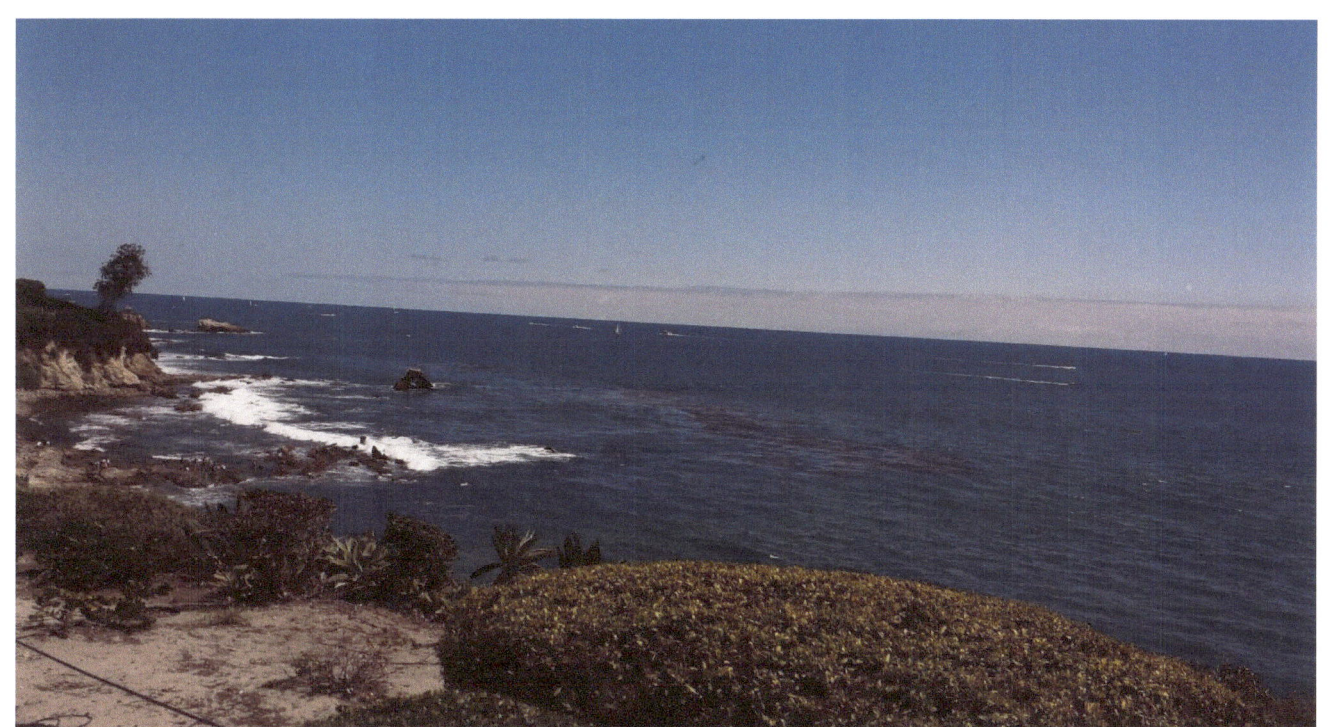

When I see your smile, I think of Love
When we hold hands, I think of Love
When I hold You, I think of Love I think of Love
When we talk, I think of Love
When we are driving, I think of Love
When I hear your voice, I think of Love I think of Love
When we are apart, I think of Love
Near or far from you, I think of Love
As we drift off to sleep. I think of Love I think of Love
When we wake up together, I think of Love
When the weather is good or bad, I think of Love
No matter where or how, I think of Love I think of Love
Love is what I think of all day and night
You are what I think of all the time
When I think of Love I think of You
When I think of You I think of Love

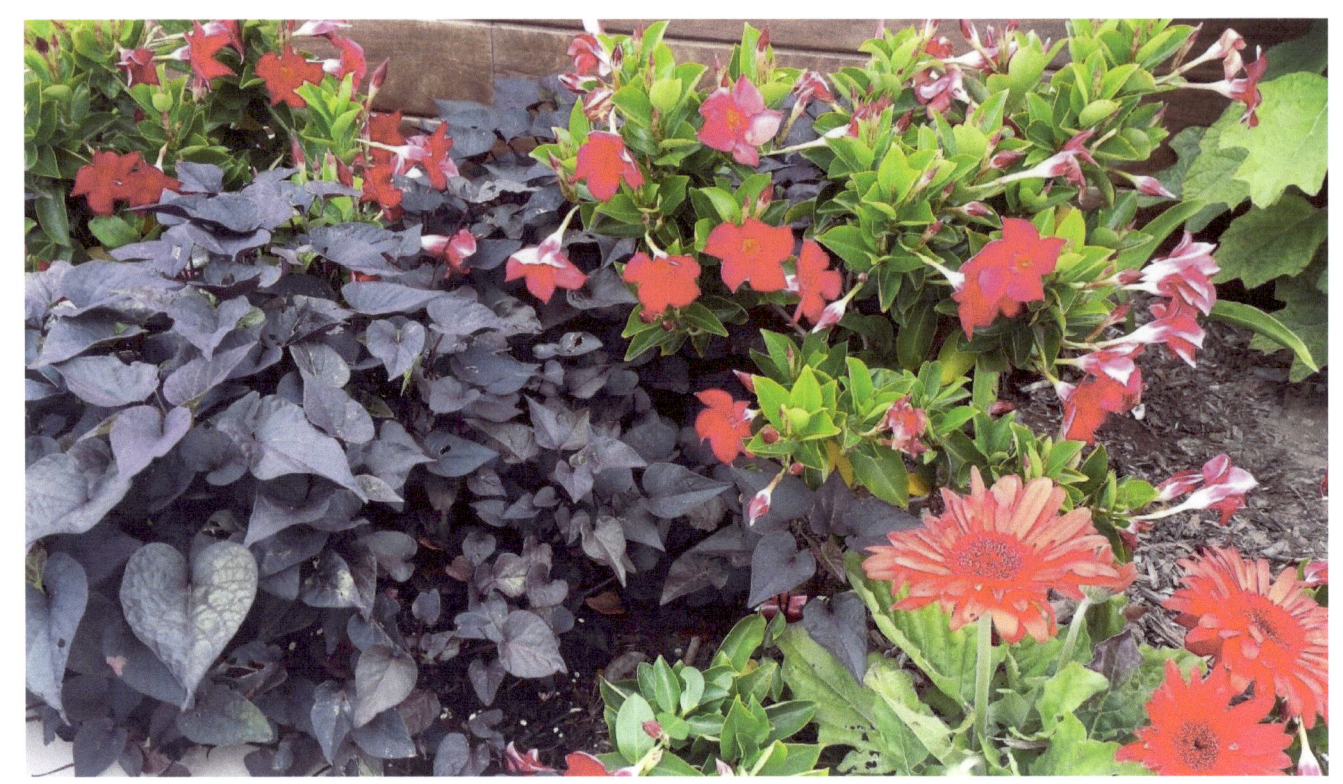

Love, you and I
Always one
together happy
man and woman
you and I
through the ages
we will be among
the most content
because of Love
you and I

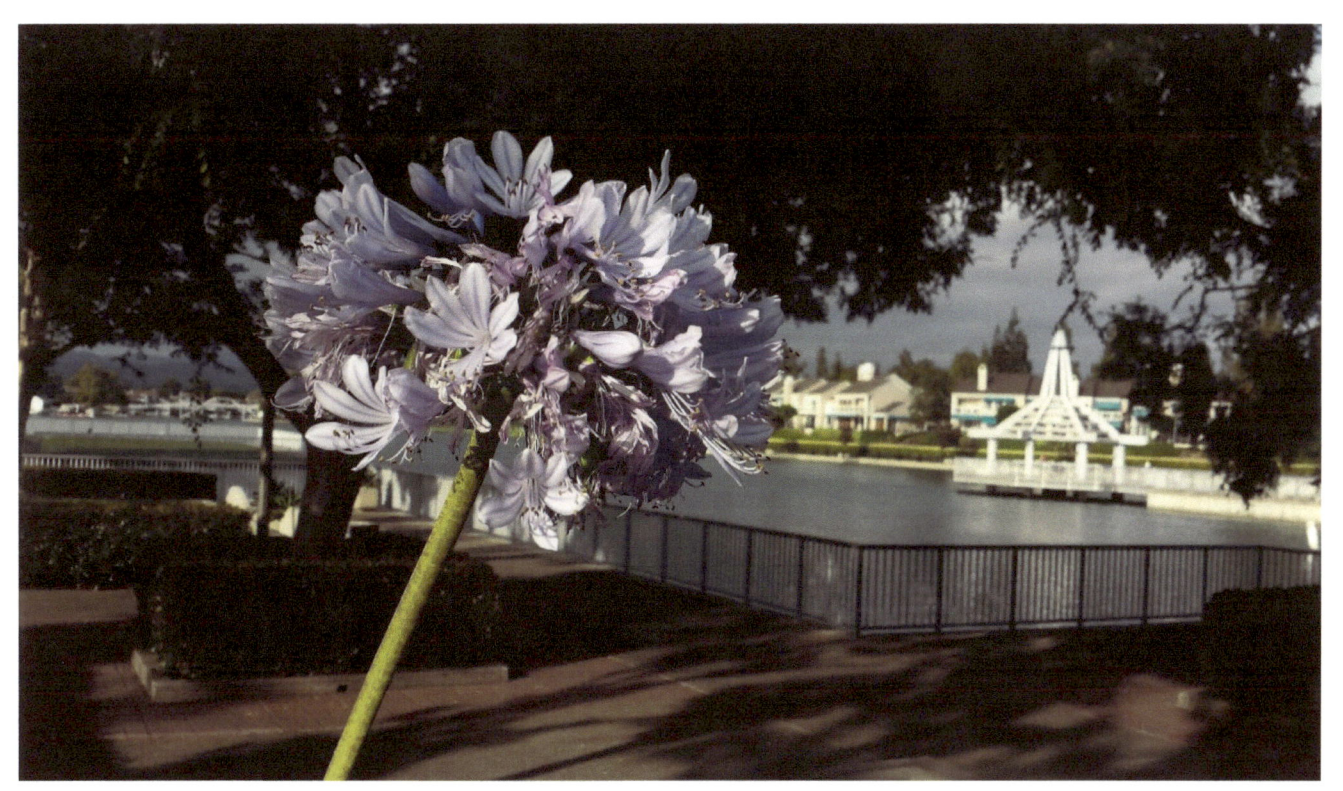

Missing you is not a problem
since I hold you so tightly in my heart
Your presence is always felt
I will though
long for your sweet full on lips kiss.

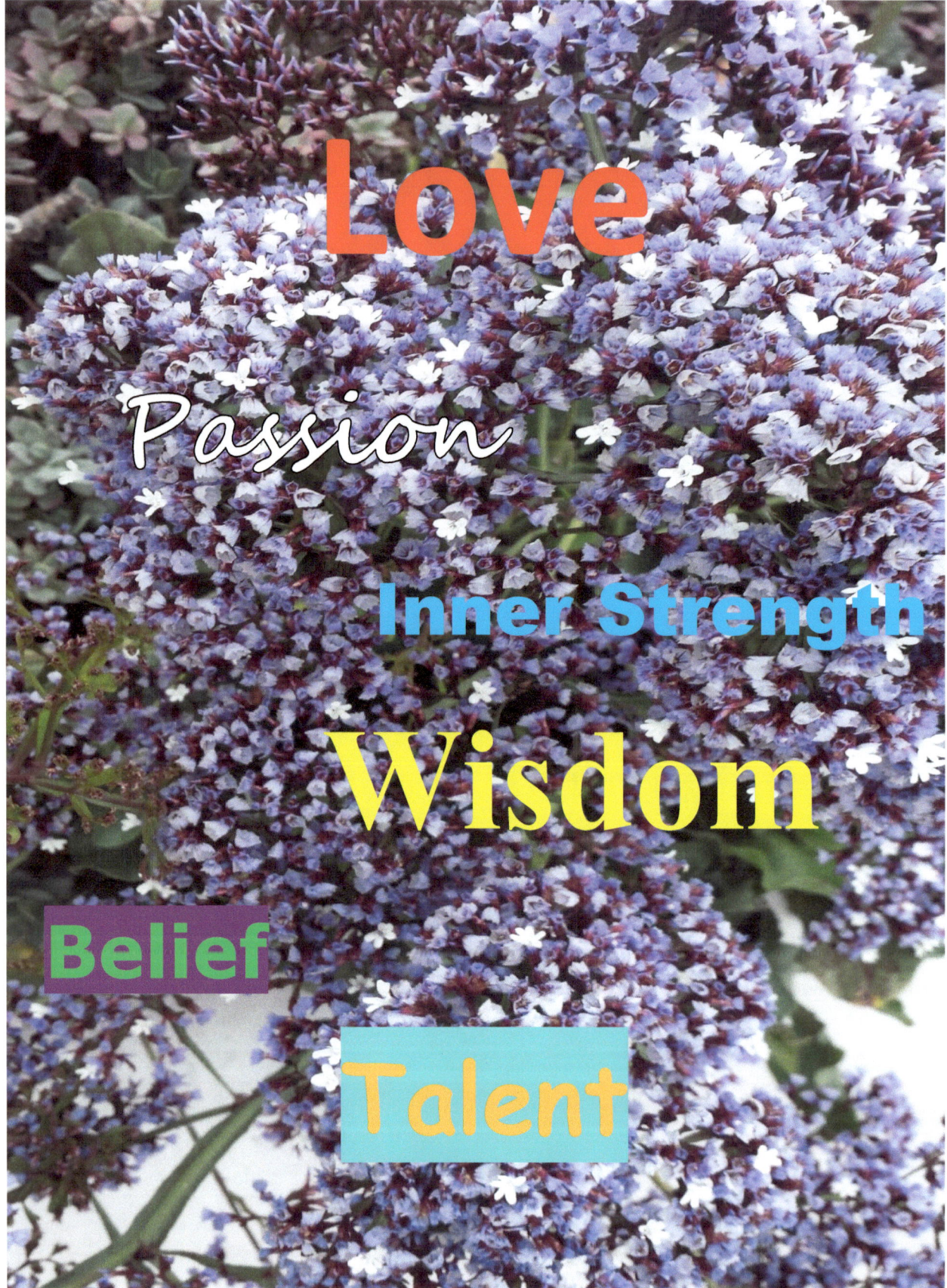

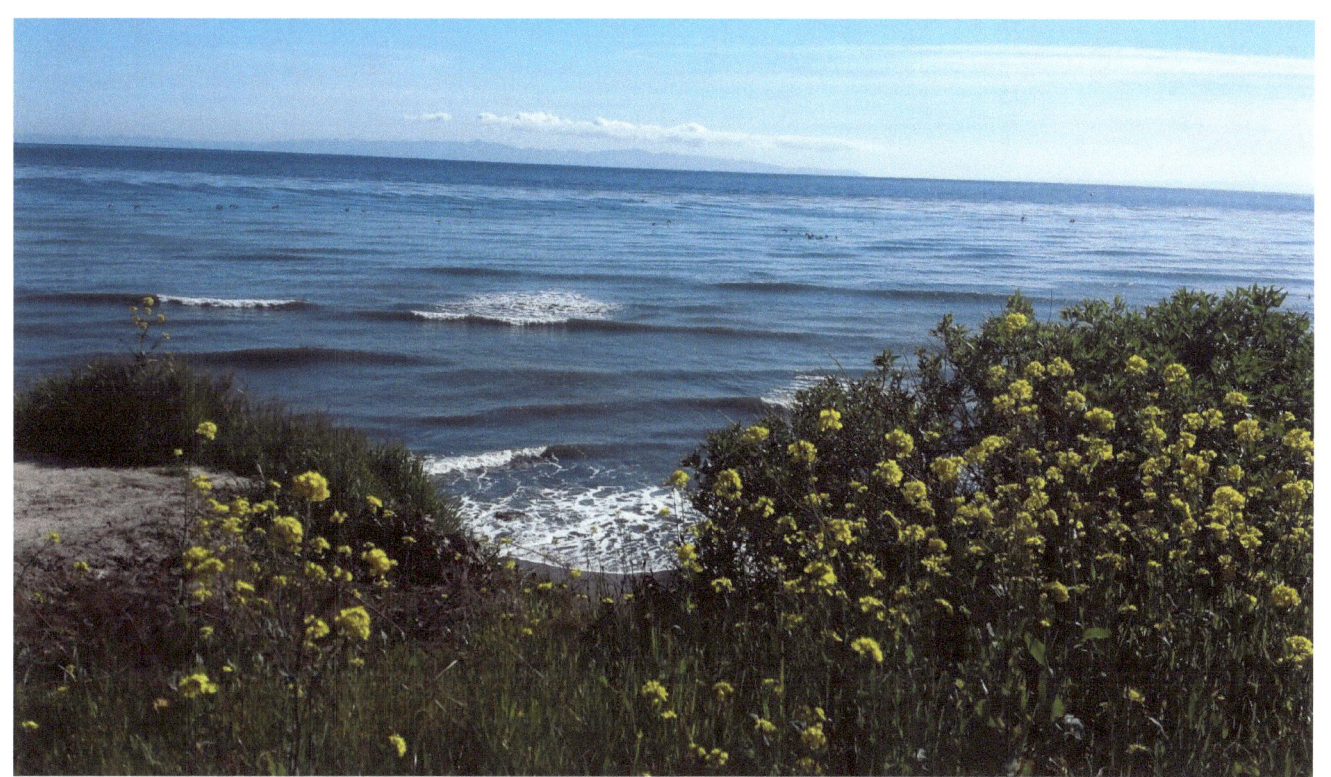

Live

and

Love

Life!

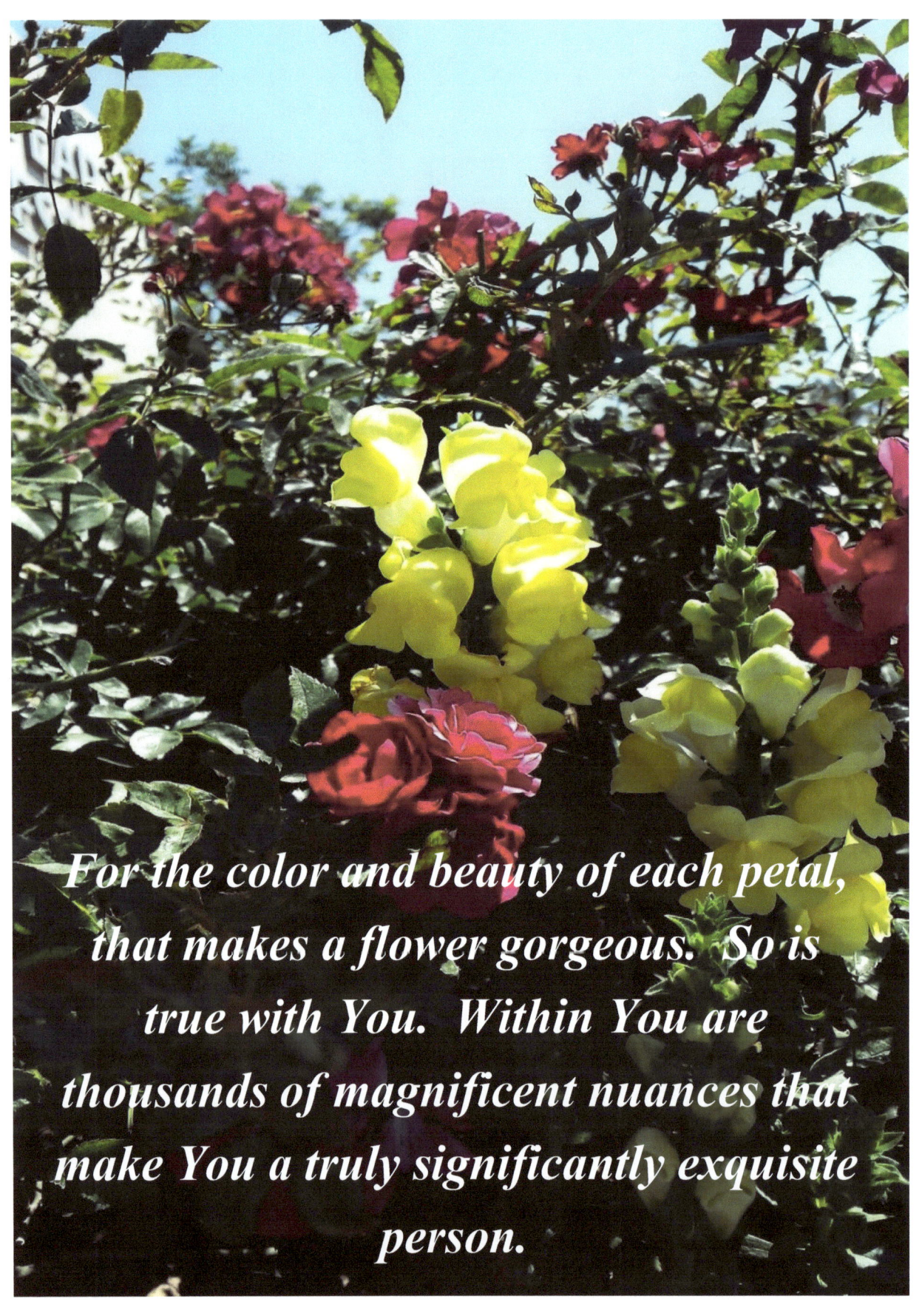

For the color and beauty of each petal, that makes a flower gorgeous. So is true with You. Within You are thousands of magnificent nuances that make You a truly significantly exquisite person.

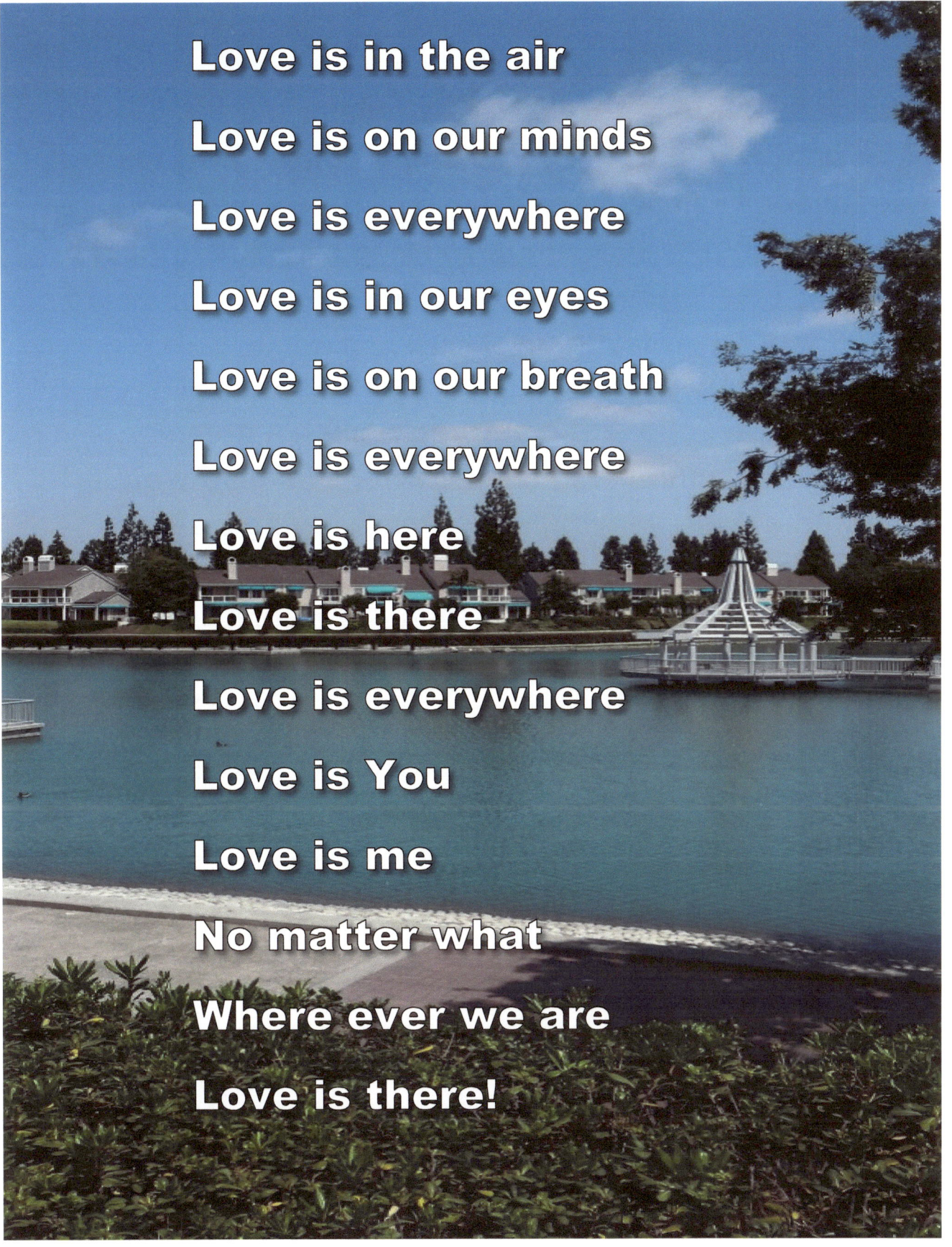

There will be no fancy words
Specially designed flowers or animals
The paper used will have no shiny Winter, Spring, Summer or Fall scenes
Descriptions, observations will ring true and honest of the way I feel and love about you
I love you for who you are
What and how you have accomplished life
A traveler, a scholar, an actor, a realist, a dreamer, a researcher, a thinker, a terrific wife, a lover, a wonderful mother, a doer, a loving daughter, a loving sister, a loving family member, a best friend, a playmate, a shoulder to cry on, a buddy to laugh with, a confidant, a partner, an individual, a soother, a fighter, a strong human being, and
a caring person to all
With these things they all spell out and conjurer up pictures of a special person
This is why I can write I LOVE YOU
On a plain piece of paper

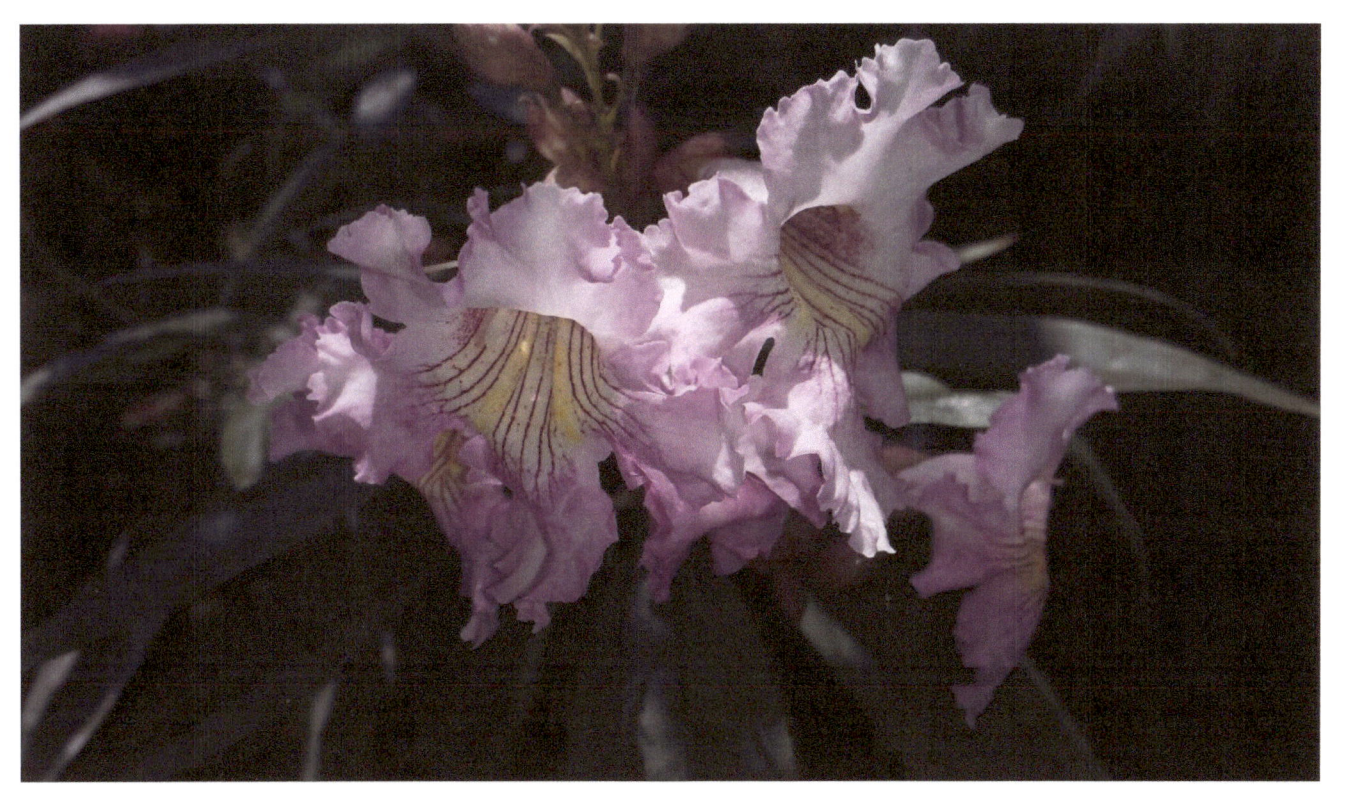

You

Make

Me

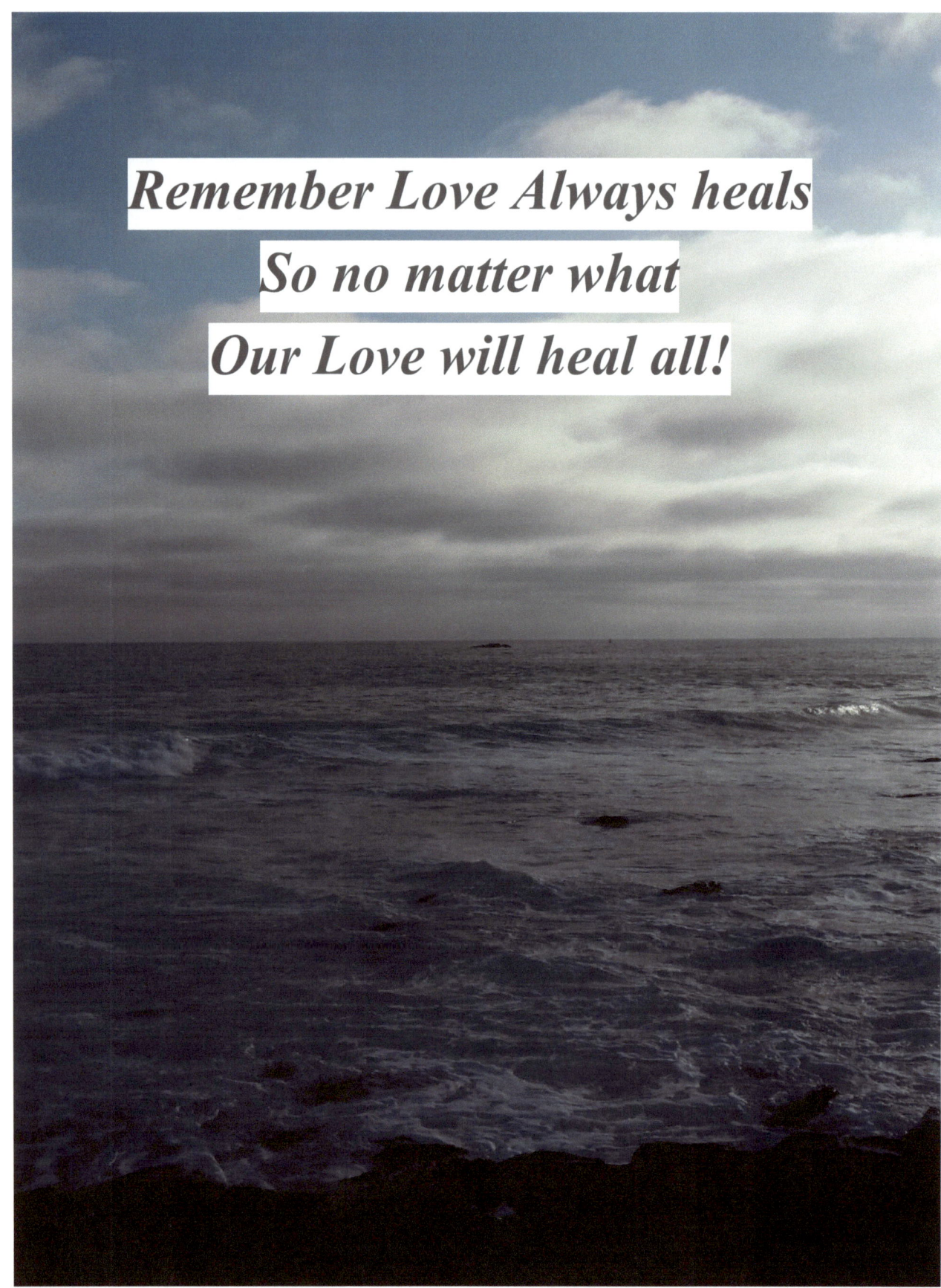

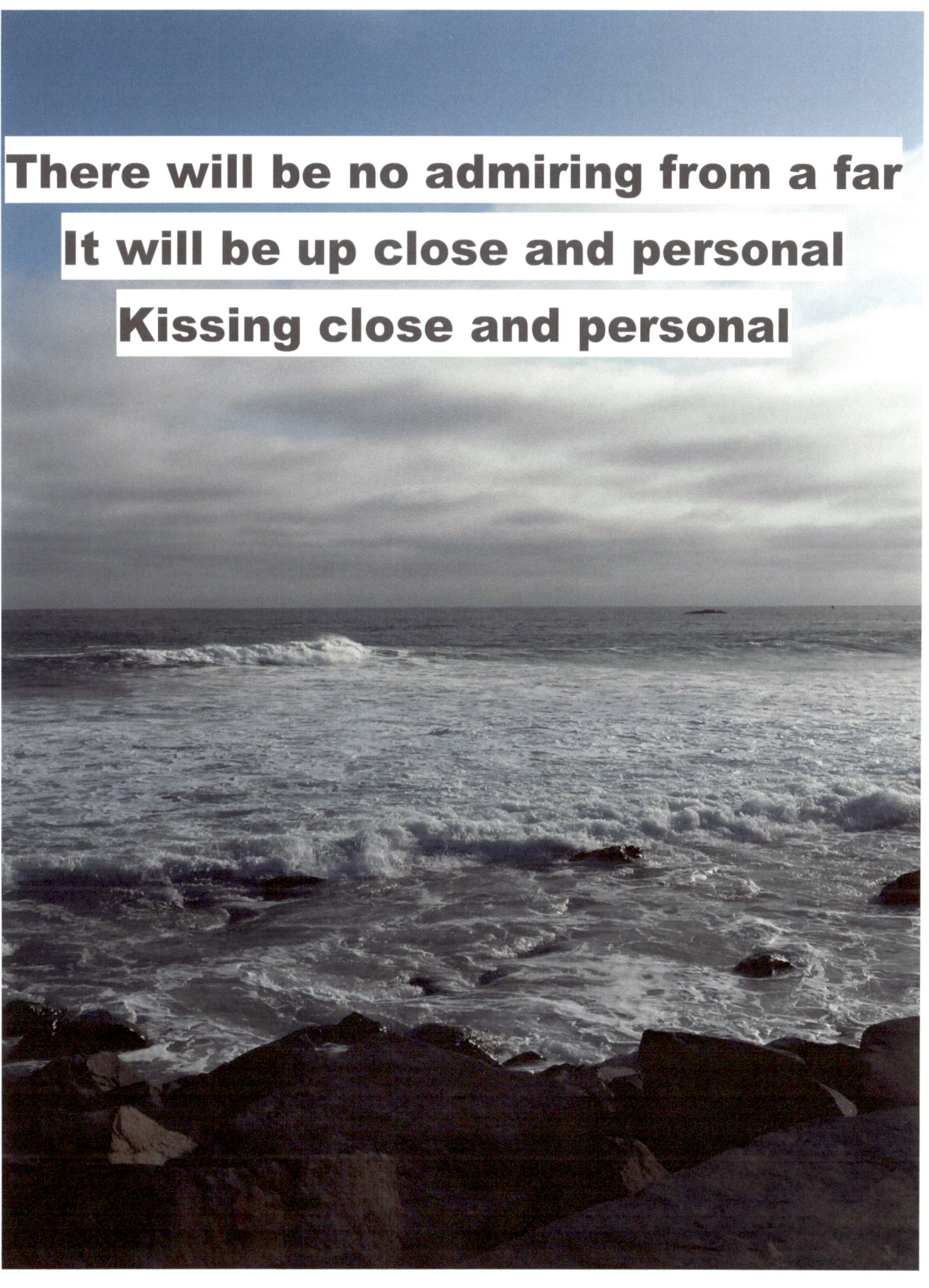

Love is our business

We work very hard

At keeping our **Love** business a success

Loving one another is a work of desire

Actually it's no work at all **Loving** you

It is a pleasure to **Love** you

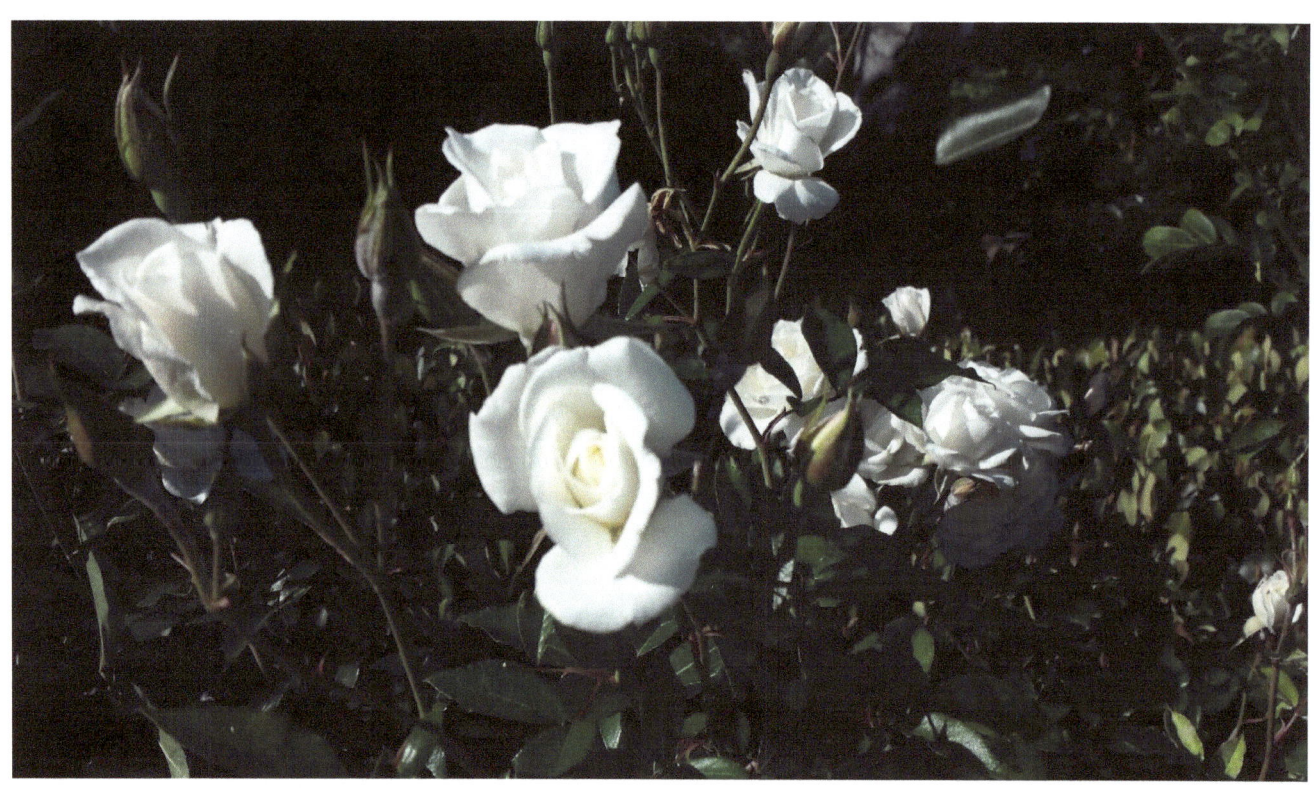

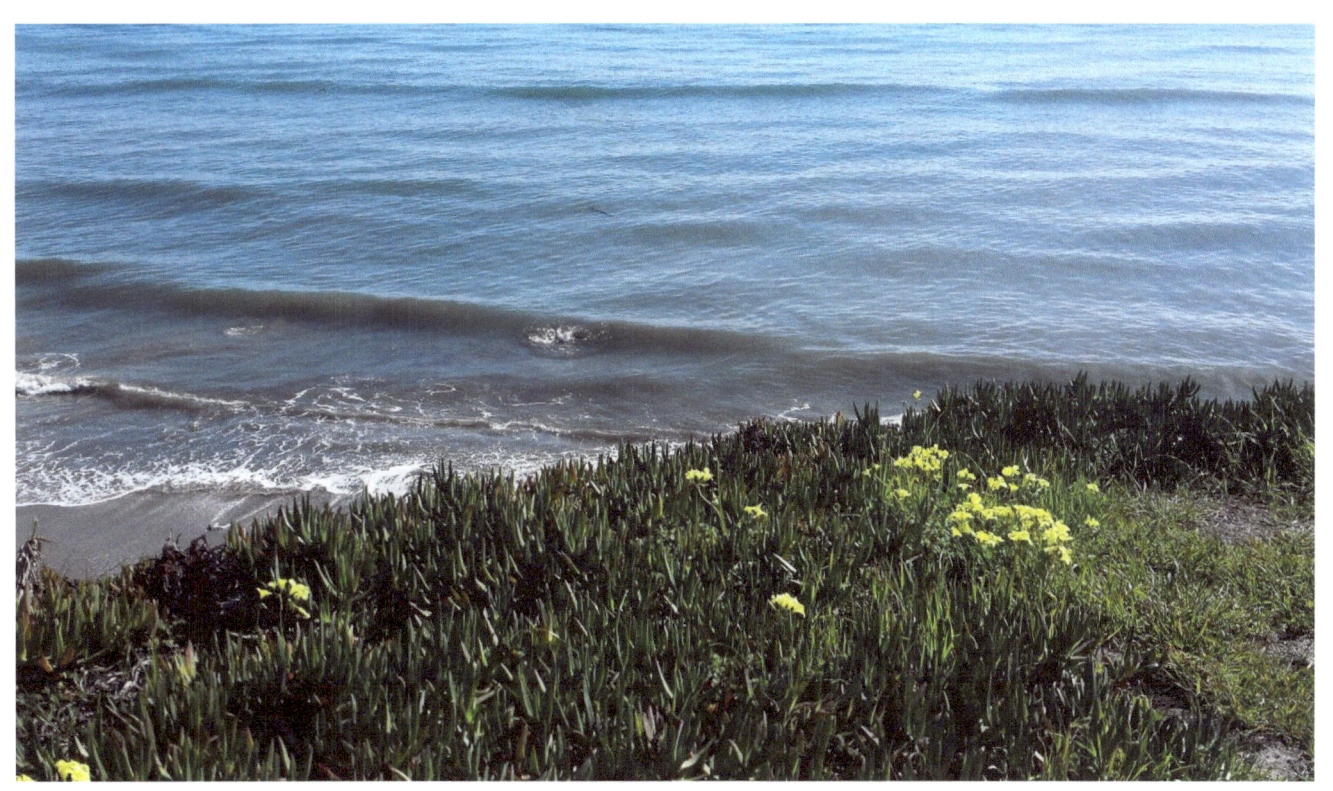

**Love is a fabulous word.
I am thrilled you are
using it on me.**

Loving you is hotsy, totsy red
At the touch it is sizzling with burning impressions
Caring is clear, baby blue
As warming as the Hawaiian islands
Feeling is sitting under a tree, soothing green
Cool breezes blowing through your hair
Sensitive is huggable, cuddly pink
With soft puppies, bunnies and ducks to hold
Happiness is lemony yellow
Fresh, clear and tranquil just as the sun burns the fog from a bay
Zeal is tangy orange
Can sting as a bee and playful like a pup
Concern is tart, plum purple
Ripe for the picking and waiting for your touch
Your emotions of love wrap me in a rainbow
Colorful, interesting lights of knowledge
Of my always being in love with you

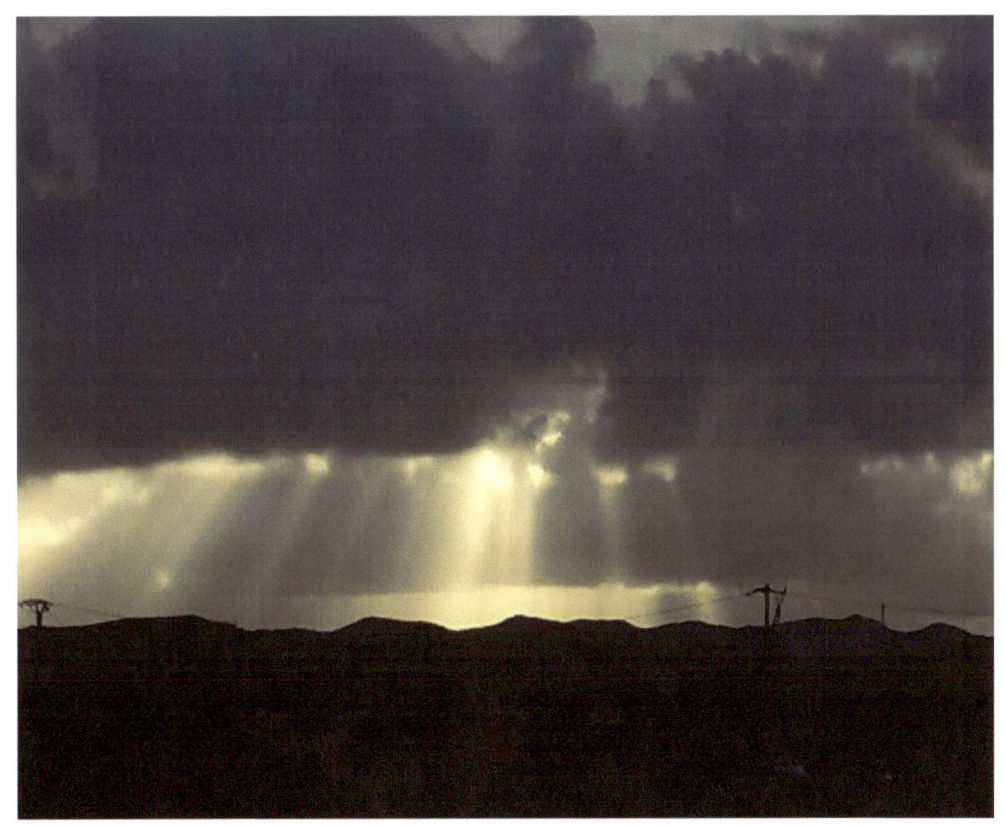

The heavens called and we listened
Coming together was our destiny
Angels assisted cupid by encircling us in love
Love is us always
God sends angels in training to watch us on how love is supposed to be
We shall be as one for always and ever
Our story is echoed through the heavens
So history can have something good to read
So continue to grasp my hand and heart
So heaven can stay in balance.

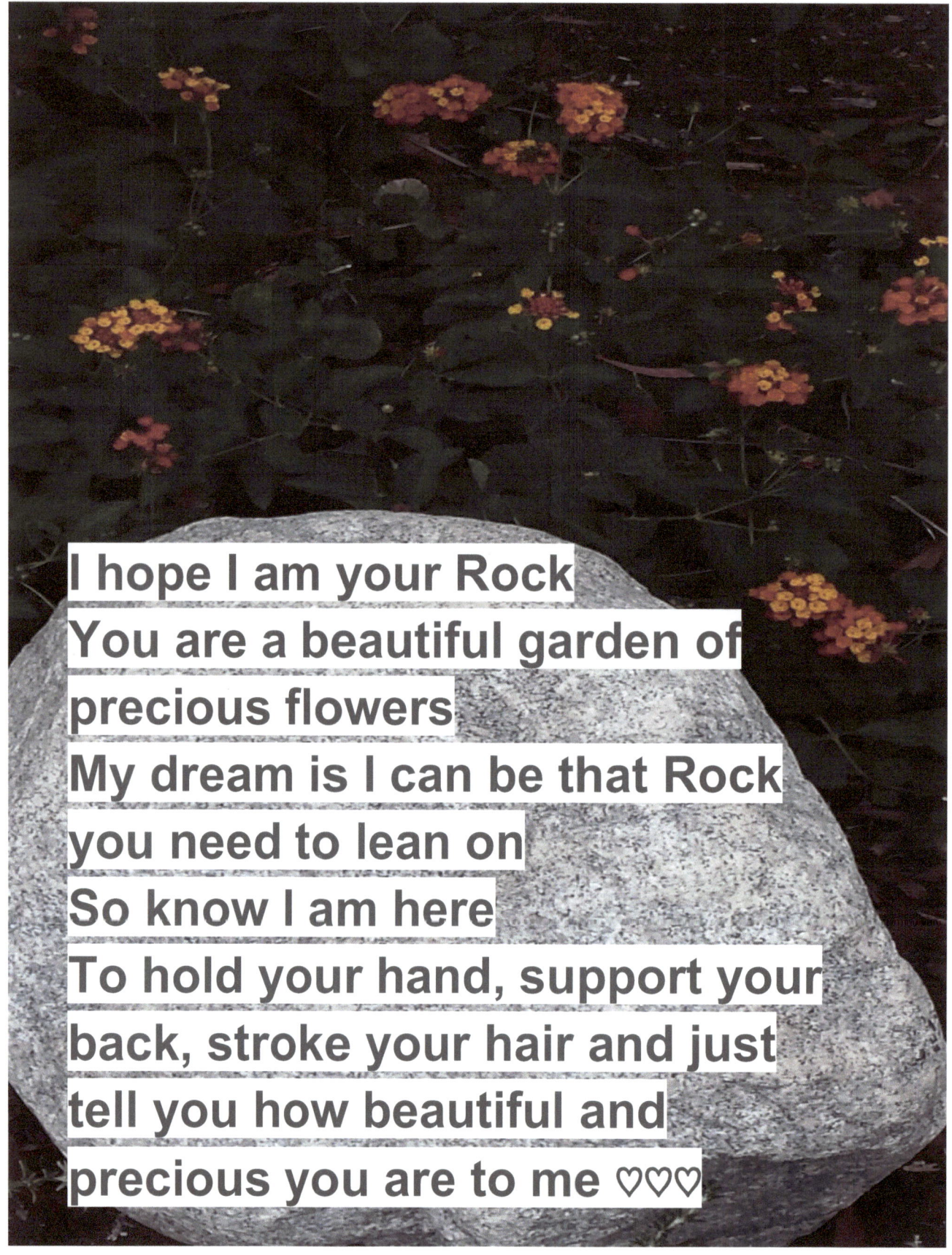

I hope I am your Rock
You are a beautiful garden of precious flowers
My dream is I can be that Rock you need to lean on
So know I am here
To hold your hand, support your back, stroke your hair and just tell you how beautiful and precious you are to me ♡♡♡

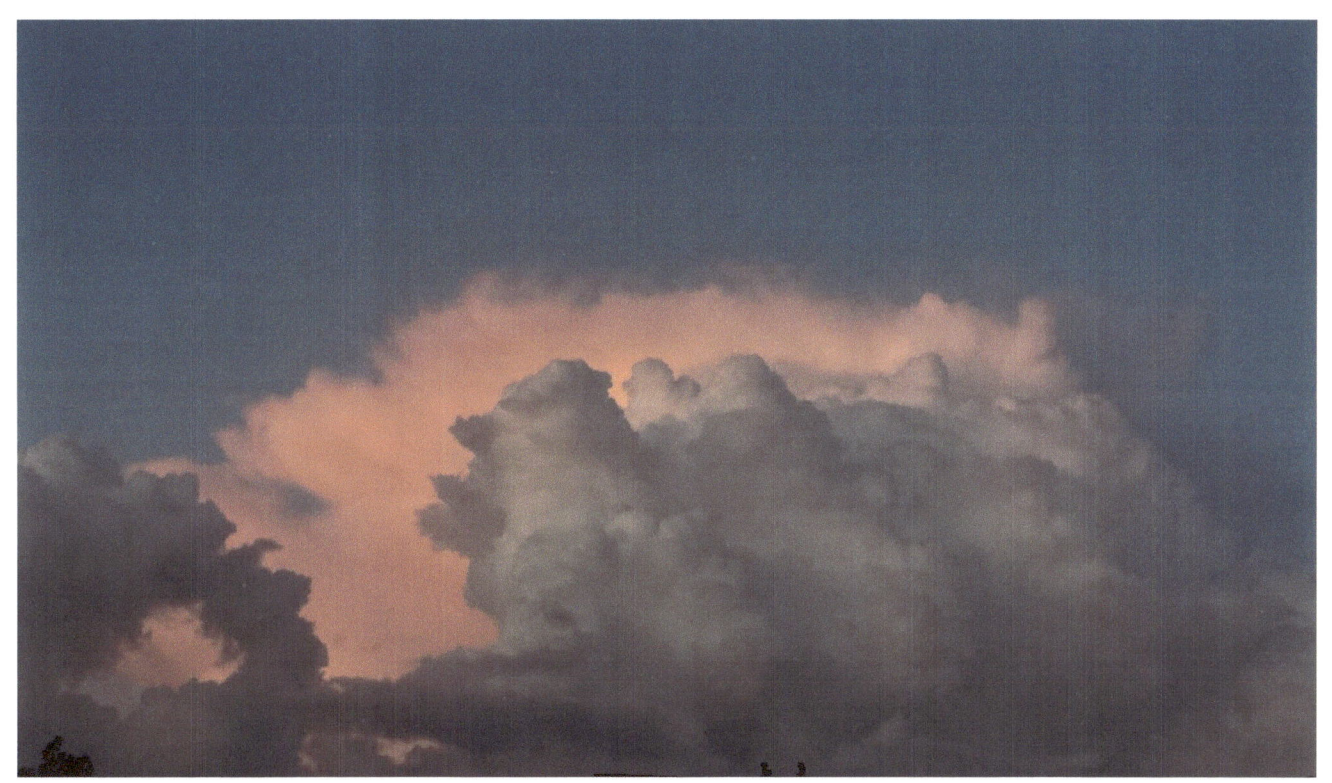

I came out of the stratosphere
Left my own planet
A strong feeling had built up in me
I was needed and would be happier else where
So I jumped into my cool sunbeam ray and shot across the galaxy
Racing towards my destiny with the wind trying to catch up
Fire in my hair and a renewed spirit in my being
I came into Earth's gravity like a falling comet
I was not falling aimlessly though
My soul knew where it was going
To find my soulmate
My future wife
A goddess on earth
The future mother to our offspring
To you my darling lovely
The holder of my heart

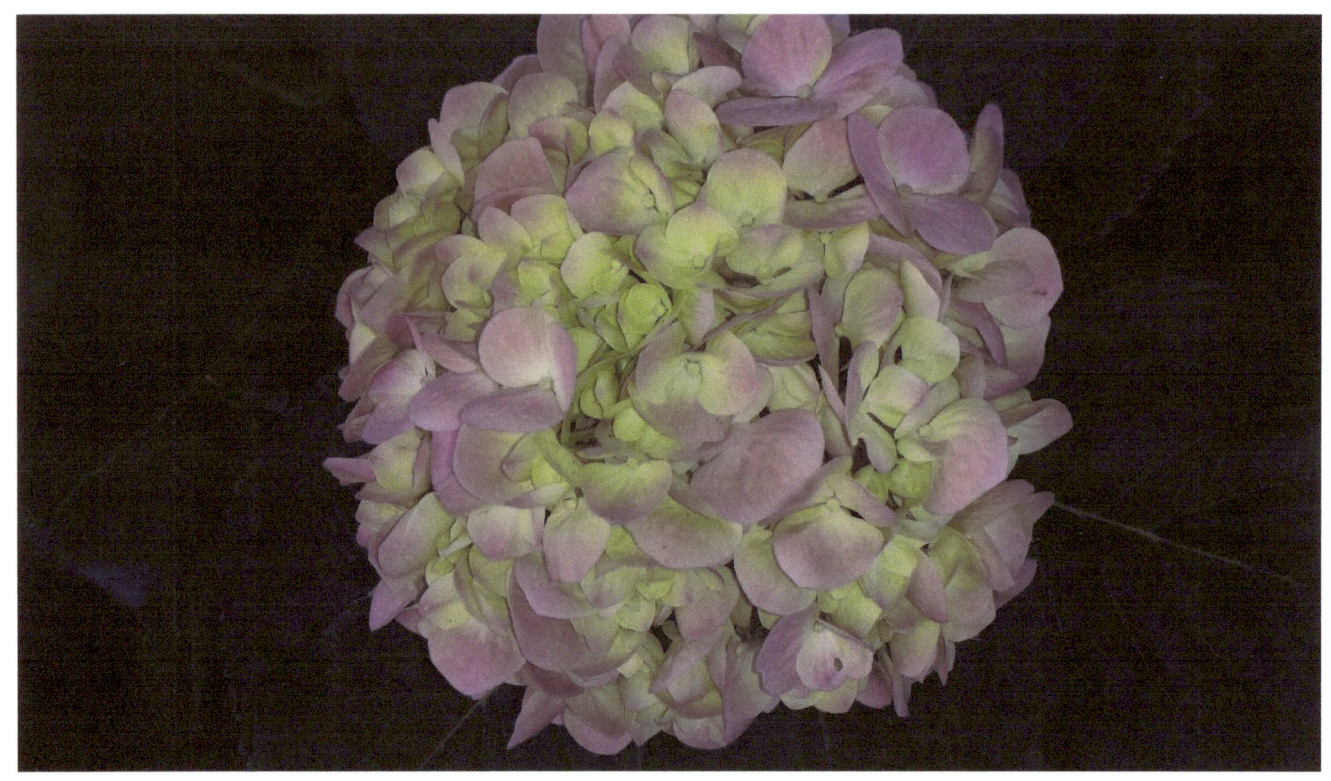

You are so delicately beautiful and you glow brighter than the sun

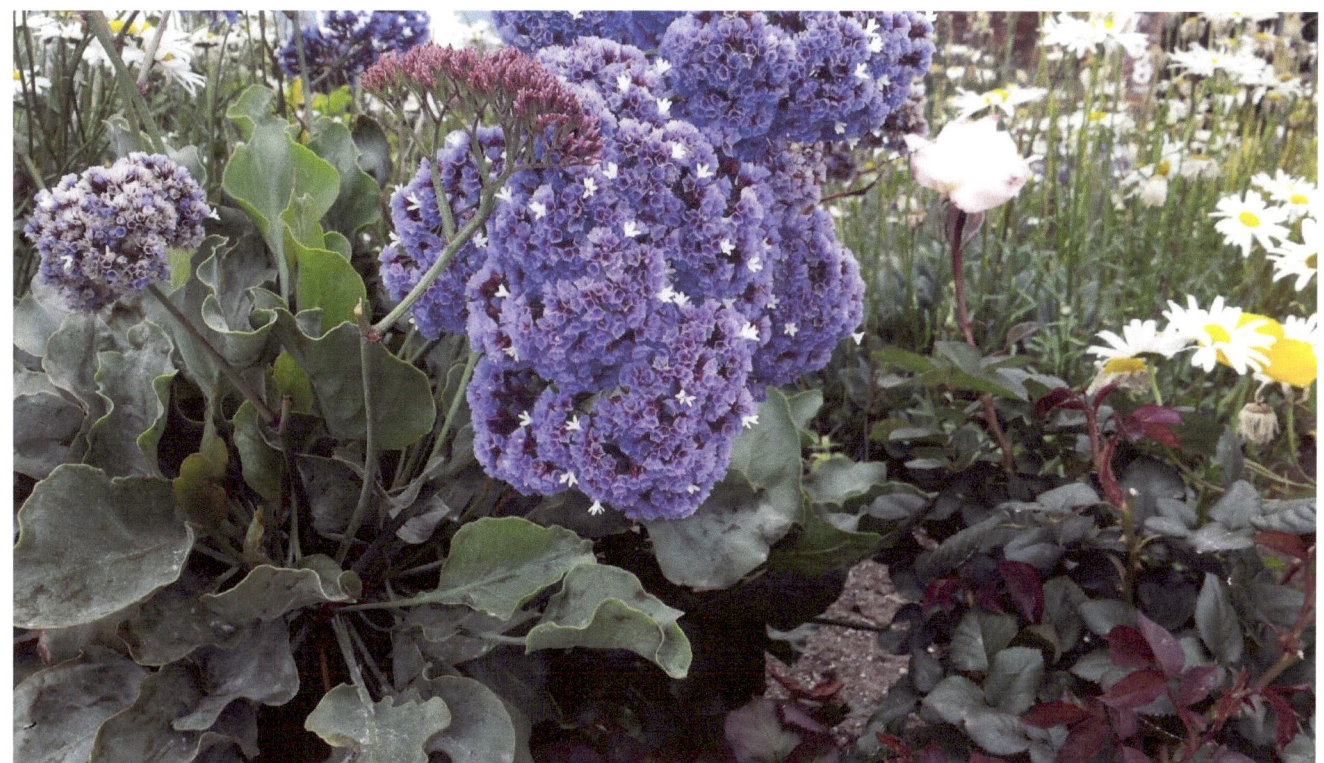

There is this story
Of a boy and a girl
But it's no ordinary story
Yes, it's of love
Not living high in the clouds
Seeing the world through pink shaded glasses love
Something more honest, enduring and true
Instead of jumping into romance
They became best friends
As time went on the boy knew she was the one
The boy asked her if they could become one
The girl excitedly agreed
Bliss and love
Have now become their words of hope

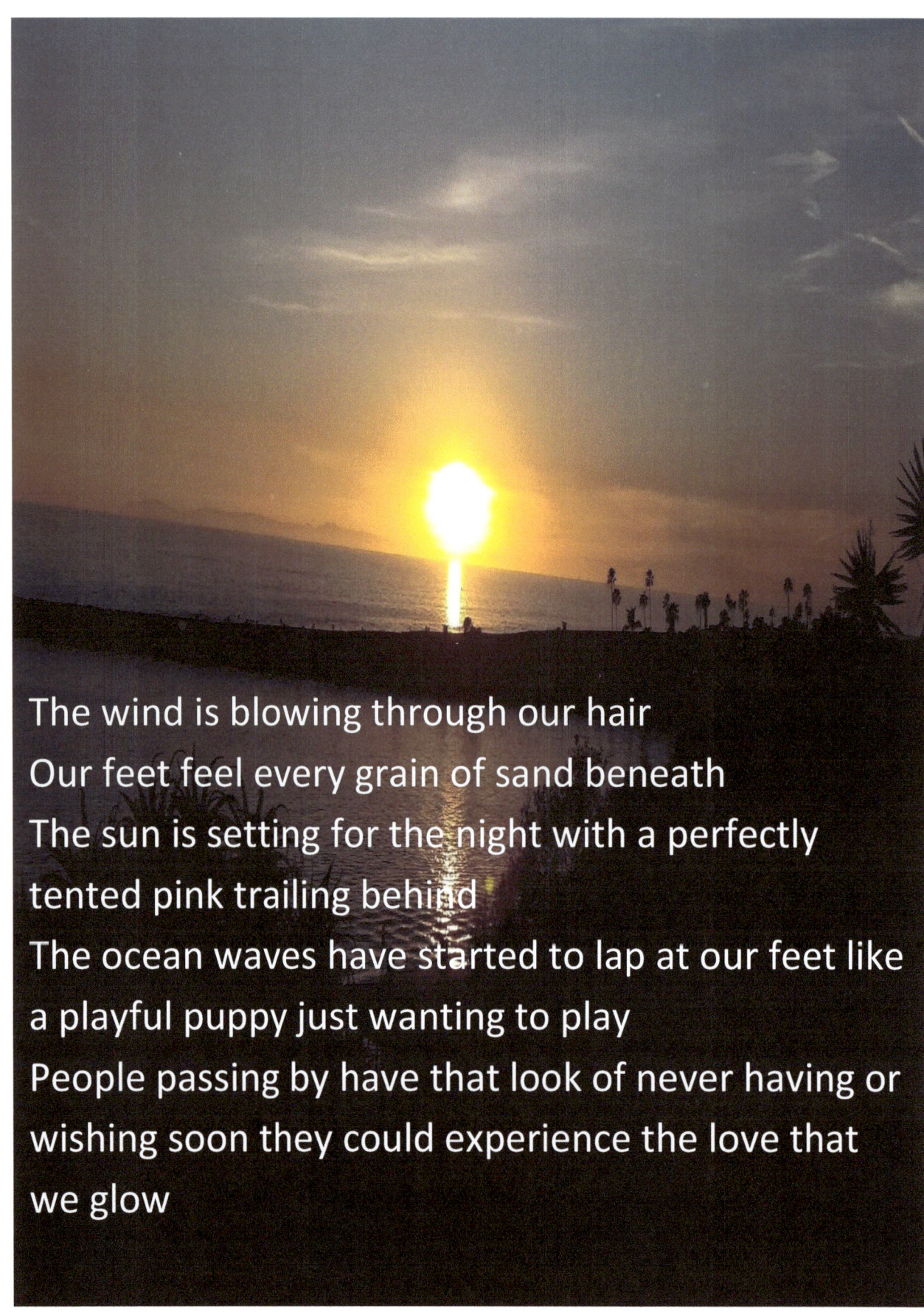

The wind is blowing through our hair
Our feet feel every grain of sand beneath
The sun is setting for the night with a perfectly tented pink trailing behind
The ocean waves have started to lap at our feet like a playful puppy just wanting to play
People passing by have that look of never having or wishing soon they could experience the love that we glow

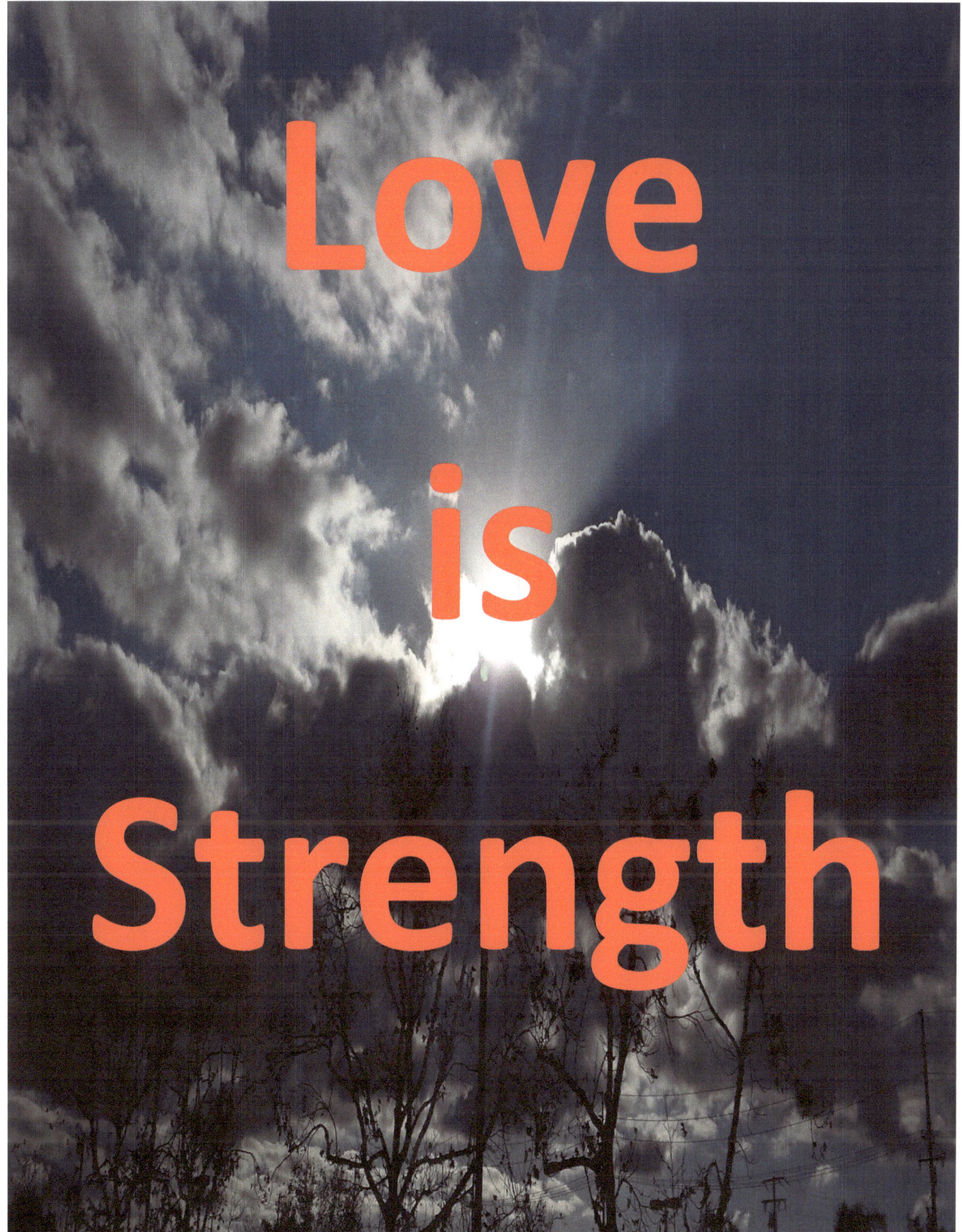

When I asked if you wanted something, I was praying you'd say, "A Kiss".

Love is long as love is sure

Love is true as love is pure

Love is wonderful as love is you

Love is terrific as love is me

Love is our life as life is our love

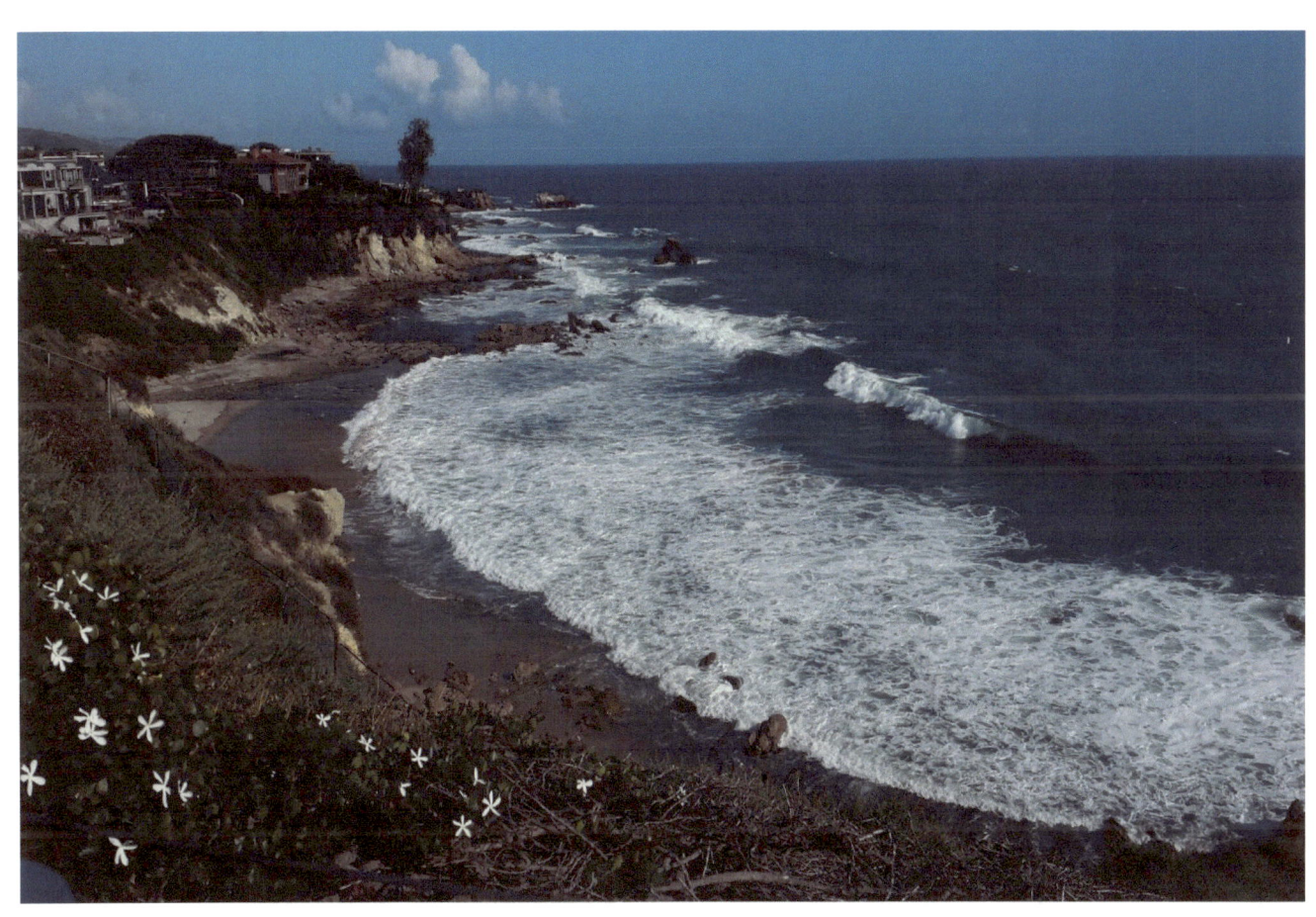

You and I, together.
They should write an opera about how endearing we are to one another.

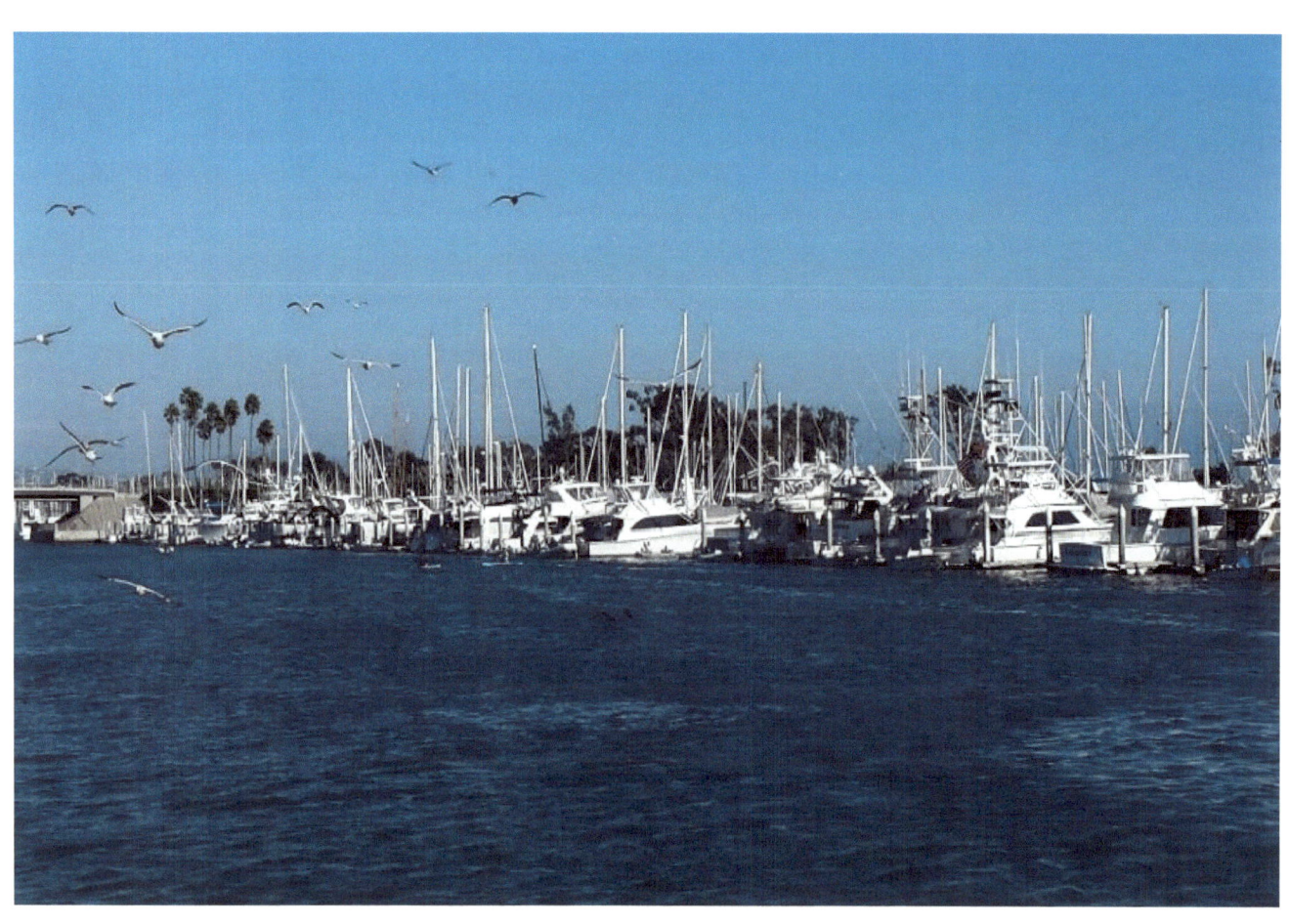

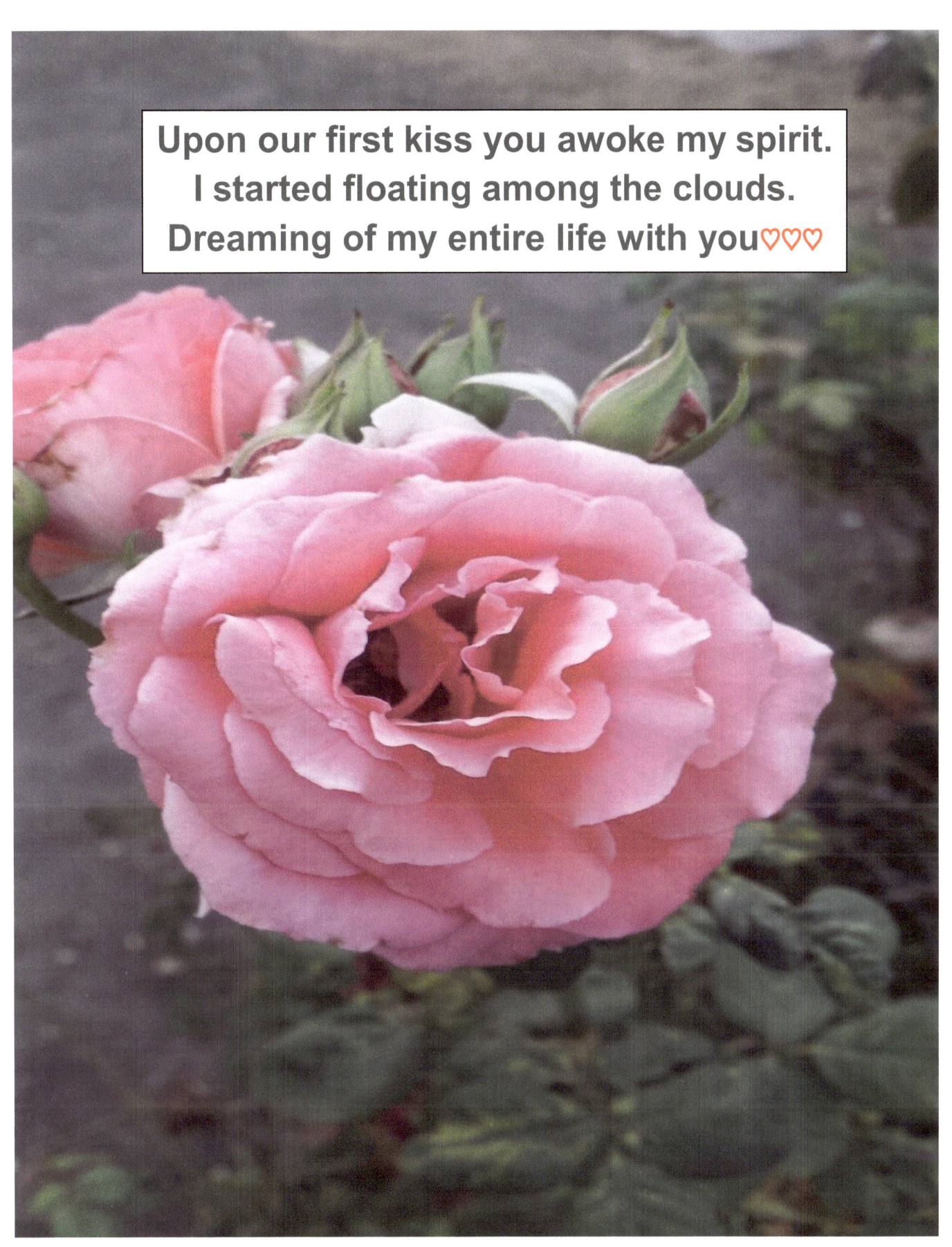

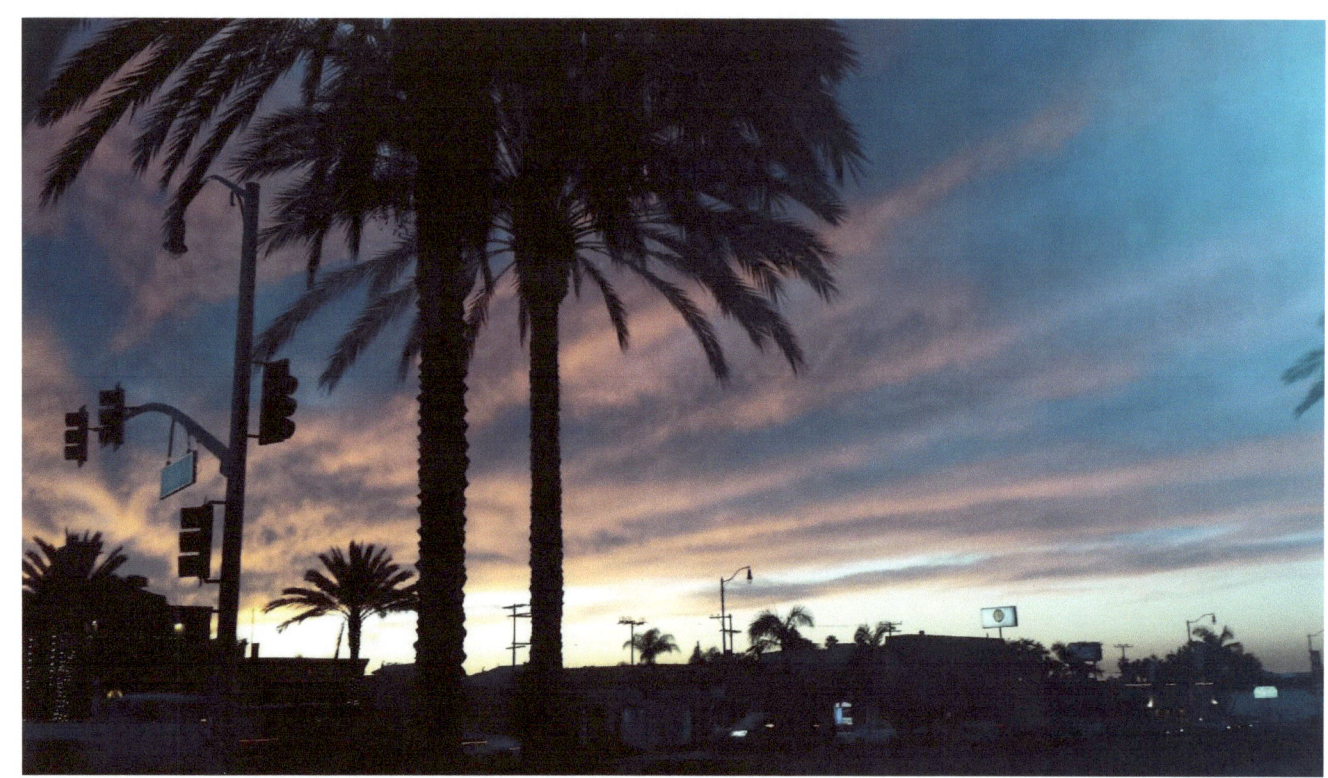

Star dust and fairy tales
Moon beams and butterfly wings
Children's smiles and kitten's purrs
Doggy tale wags and birdie whistles
Bunnies pink noses and dolphins eyes gleaming
Among these and a million more sweet details
This is you
All wrapped up in a pretty pink bow.

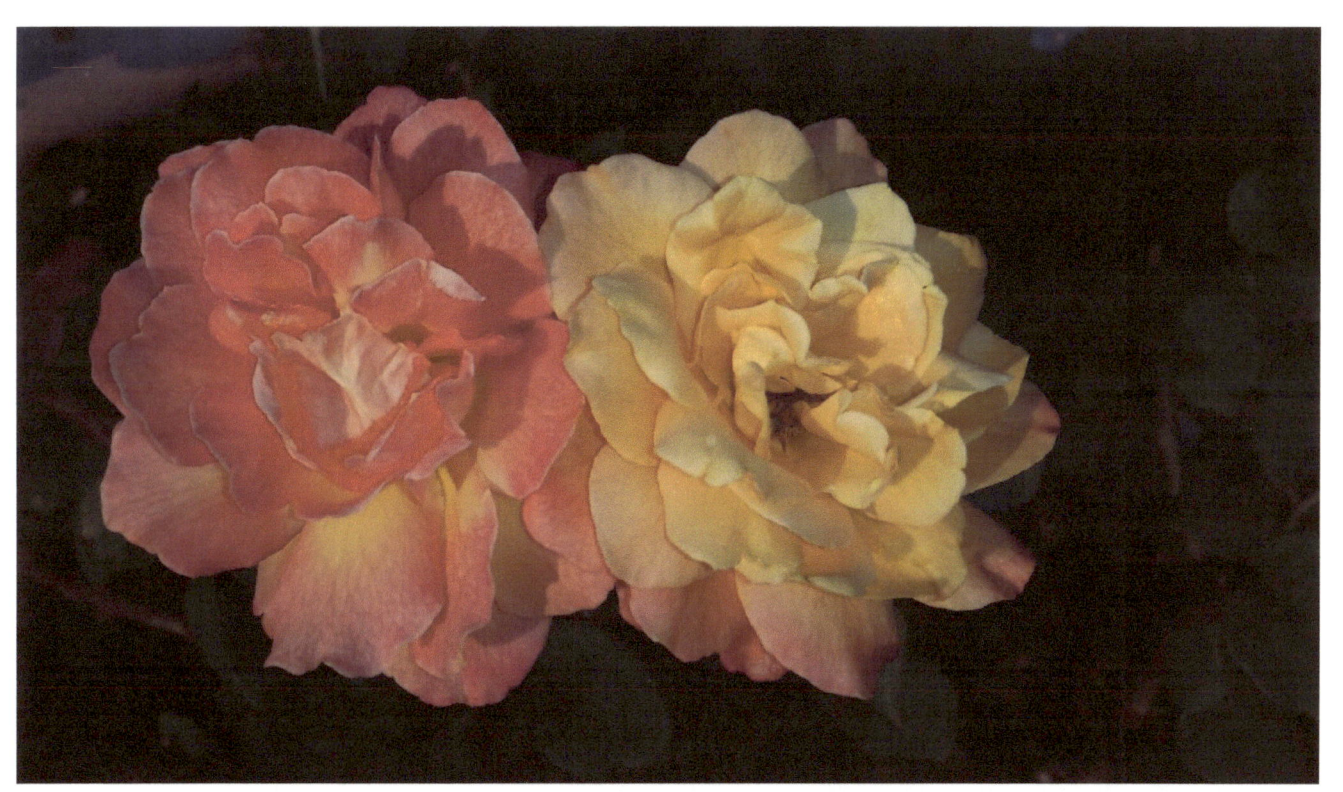

Intertwined our love has become

It is not merely I am you and you are me

Or that where you scratch I itch

You feel pain when I hurt

I am joyous when you succeed

Our love is just that

We are love

So when we say we love one another

We are saying

Our names as we now know it

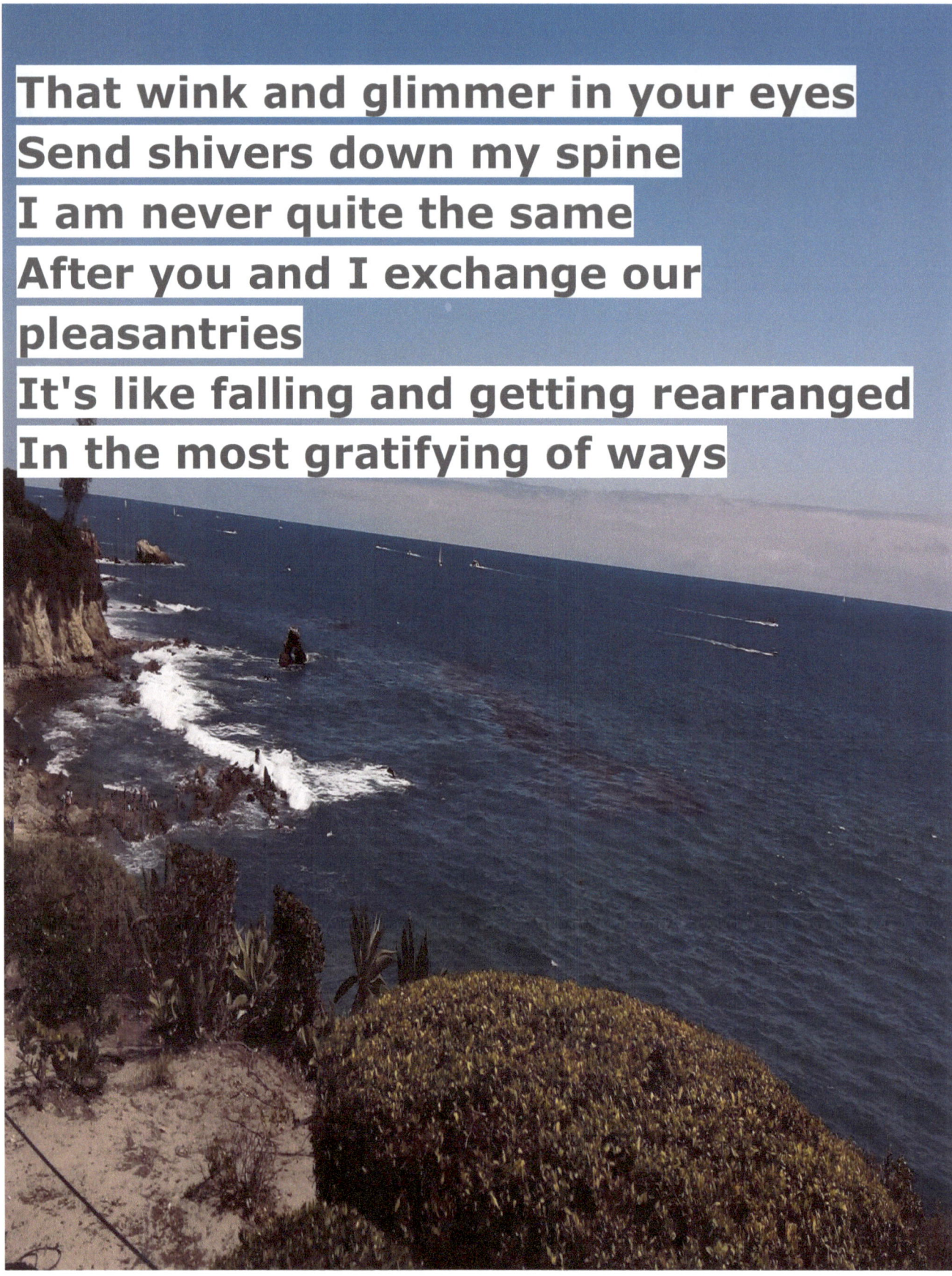

That wink and glimmer in your eyes
Send shivers down my spine
I am never quite the same
After you and I exchange our pleasantries
It's like falling and getting rearranged
In the most gratifying of ways

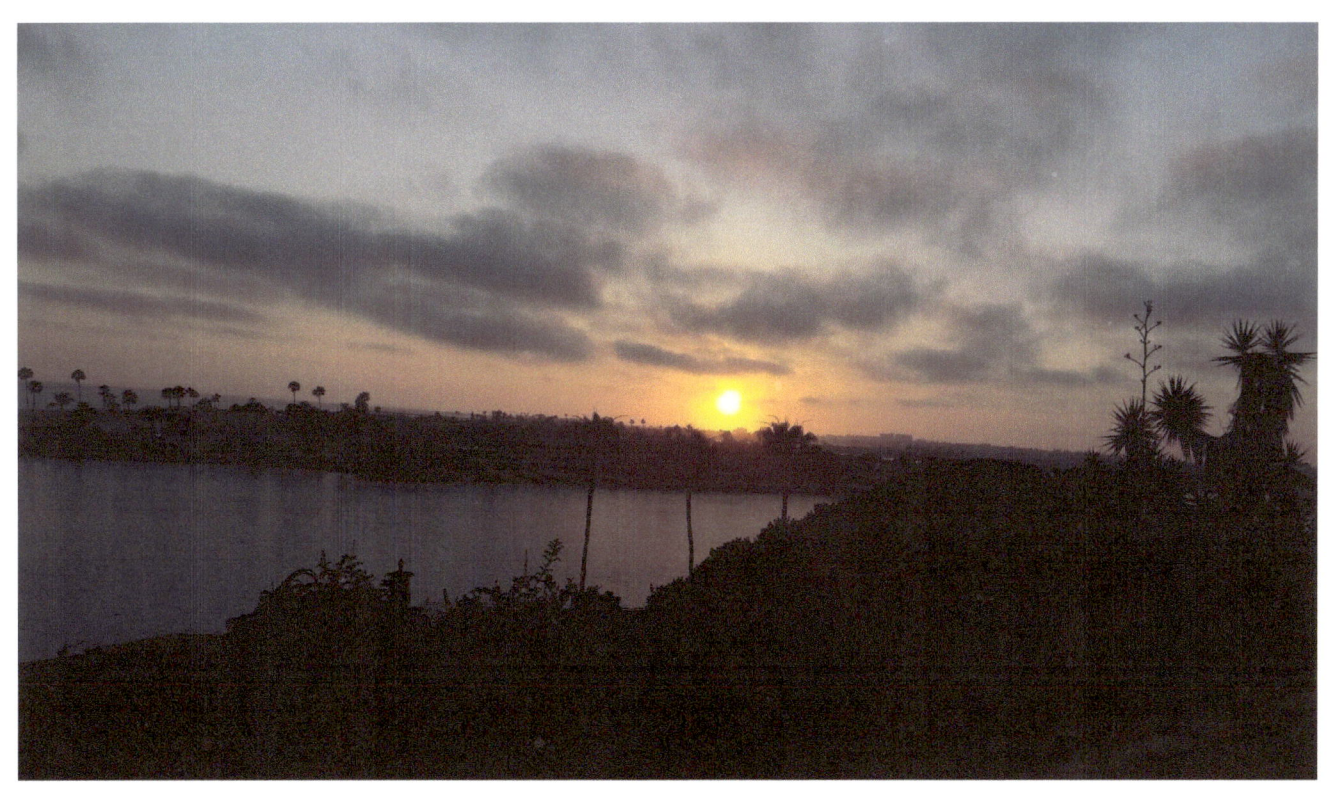

Love is like the sun coming out from behind the mountains. One of the most awesomely poetic scenes and feelings ever known. That is my life with you. ♡♡♡

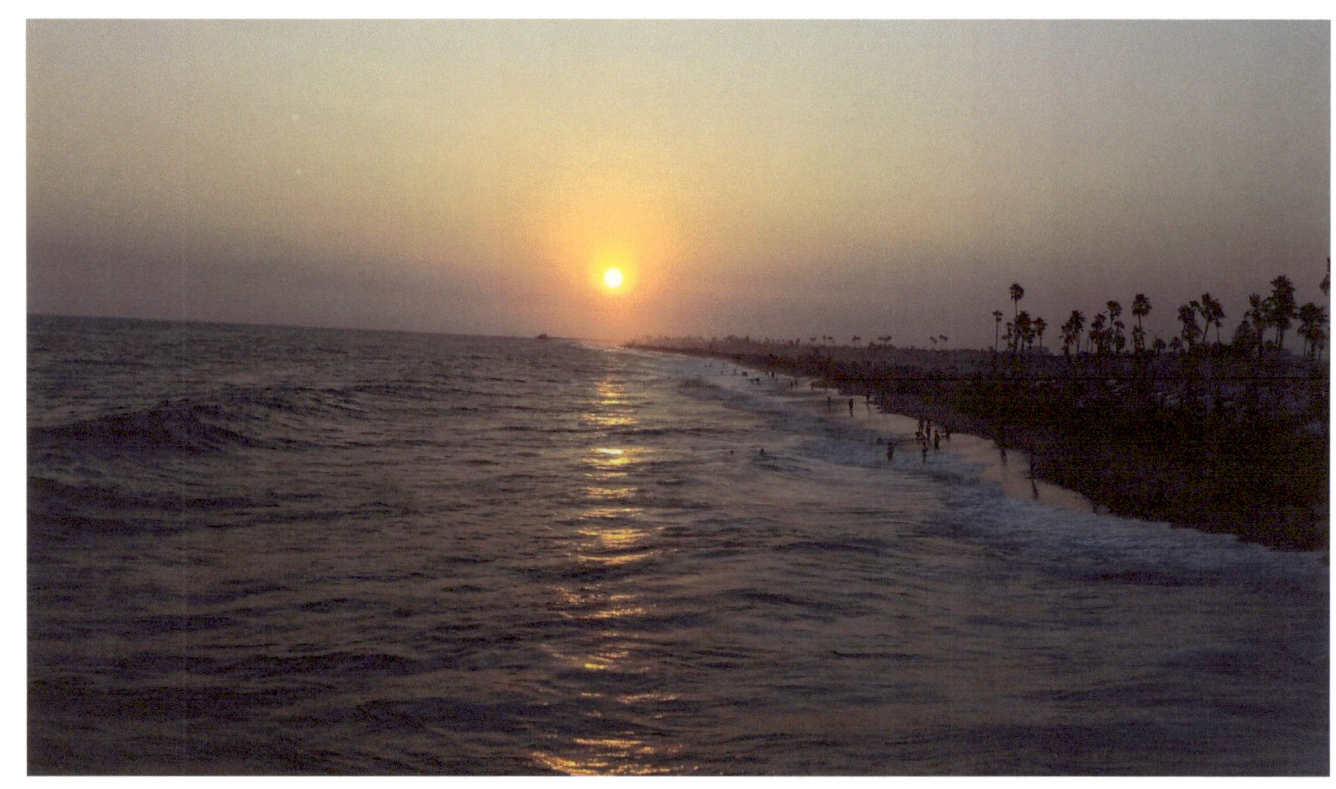

Three things will last forever - faith, hope, and love - and the greatest of these is love.

1 Corinthians 13:13

My Lovely Girl!

My Lovely Girl!

My Lovely Girl!

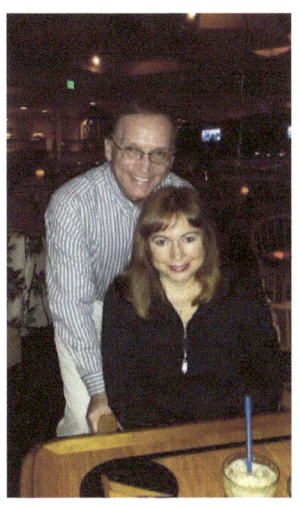

The Warmest of Wishes,

Bonnie and John Scott Hightower

Other books by Bonnie and John Scott Hightower:

<u>You are my Always!</u> - **A Romantic Poetry book**

<u>Counting to 10 Ten with Buddy and Oscar</u> -**A Children's book**

<u>Halloween Pumpkin, where are you?</u> - **A Children's book**

<u>Santa, where are you?</u> - **A Children's book**

<u>Eastern Bunny, where are you?</u> - **A Children's book**

<u>Have an Adventurous Day!</u> - **A Children's book**

Available on Amazon.com

My Lovely Girl!

The Warmest of Wishes,

Bonnie and John Scott Hightower

Follow us at:

John Scott Hightower @gladwethoughtof

art_gladwethoughtofit John Scott Hightower

Glad We Thought Of It John Scott Hightower

and our web site.

familyhightower.wixsite.com/website

www.ingramcontent.com/pod-product-compliance
Lightning Source LLC
Chambersburg PA
CBHW041932240526
45473CB00034B/927